RECIPES FOR
MINDFULNESS
IN YOUR LIBRARY

RECIPES for
Mindfulness in Your Library
Supporting Resilience
and Community Engagement

EDITED BY

Madeleine Charney, Jenny Colvin,
and Richard Moniz

ALA
Editions

Chicago   2019

Extensive effort has gone into ensuring the reliability of the information in this book; however, the publisher makes no warranty, express or implied, with respect to the material contained herein.

ISBN: 978-0-8389-1783-1 (paper)

Library of Congress Cataloging-in-Publication Data

Names: Charney, Madeleine, editor. | Colvin, Jenny, editor. | Moniz, Richard, editor.
Title: Recipes for mindfulness in your library : supporting resilience and community engagement / edited by Madeleine Charney, Jenny Colvin, and Richard Moniz.
Description: Chicago : ALA Editions, An imprint of the American Library Association, 2019. | Includes index.
Identifiers: LCCN 2018046682 | ISBN 9780838917831 (print : alk. paper)
Subjects: LCSH: Public services (Libraries)—Psychological aspects. | Mindfulness (Psychology) | Mindfulness (Psychology)—Study and teaching. | Libraries and community—United States—Case studies. | Librarians—Psychology.
Classification: LCC Z711 .R327 2019 | DDC 025.501/9—dc23 LC record available at https://lccn.loc.gov/2018046682

Cover design by Karen Sheets de Gracia. Cover image © JAKKAPAN JABJAINAI. Interior design and composition by Dianne M. Rooney using Brandon Grotesque and Bookman Old Style typefaces.

♾ This paper meets the requirements of ANSI/NISO Z39.48–1992 (Permanence of Paper).

Printed in the United States of America

23 22 21 20 19   5 4 3 2 1

Contents

Acknowledgments   ix
Introduction xi

PART I ■ Library as Hub

1   Cultivating a "Mindful Medicine" Ethos   3
Rebecca Snyder and Robin O'Hanlon

2   Accidentally Sustainable   9
Building a Weekly Meditation Community
Laura Horwood-Benton

3   The Be Project   17
Sparking a Quiet Revolution in Rural Kentucky
Katie Scherrer

4   Providing a Space to Rest   23
Weaving Restorative Yoga into the Strategic Plan
Millie Jackson

PART II ■ Innovative Services

5 **Mindful McQuade**   29
Mindfulness in the Heart of a Small College Campus
Catherine Wong, Katherine LaFlamme, and Michaela Keating

6 **Mindfulness Experiences**   37
The Library Brain Booth
Katia G. Karadjova

7 **Craving Quiet**   45
A Library's Zen Zone
Kellie Sparks and Hillary Fox

PART III ■ Personal Practice

8 **Mindful and Reflective Writing as Strategy**   55
How a Work Journal Can Help Make You Whole
Michelle Reale

9 **Mindfulness Is Not a Life Hack**   61
Elizabeth Galoozis and Caro Pinto

10 **Outreach for Inreach**   67
Using Digital Resources to Promote Mindfulness
Jenn Carson

11 **Mindfully Managing Library Teams**   75
Jenny Colvin

PART IV ▪ Teaching/Research

12 Shifting the Pace   83

Contemplative Practices and the Research Process

Lisa Meléndez

13 A Persistent Praxis   91

Putting Mindfulness Scholarship into Action
at Minneapolis College

Jennifer Sippel

14 Going with the Flow   99

Finding Flexible *Fun*ctionality in Teaching and
Mentoring

Anne Pemberton and Lisa Coats

15 Overcoming Research Anxiety   105

A Mindful Approach to Literature Review Searching

Elizabeth Galoozis and Kevin Michael Klipfel

Contributors 113
Index 119

Acknowledgments

We would like to give special thanks to our editor, Jamie Santoro, and her talented and dedicated associates at ALA, especially Angela Gwizdala. We would also like to thank our authors for sharing their stories and everyone out there in the profession shaping libraries to be more mindful, caring, and compassionate places.

Introduction

Mindfulness (e.g., meditation, movement, reflective writing, engaged listening) is a powerful way to build personal and community resilience. In challenging times of rapid social change and uncertainty, mindfulness offers vital life skills that librarians can offer their users and harness for our own self-care and cultivation of joy. Mindfulness experiences can also be structured to support social justice efforts, nurturing community engagement and civil discourse.

This collection of stories—recipes, if you will—explore a wide range of approaches in which librarians integrate mindfulness into their teaching, collections, services,programming, spaces, partnerships, and professional development.

Not simply a set of techniques, mindfulness offered in libraries ideally stems from the personal practice of the librarian designing and implementing these offerings. Our hope is that this foundation also be present in administrators, who can then encourage mindfulness for their staff and patrons. From this place of authenticity, our shared leadership in this burgeoning movement will take root with credibility and lasting value.

As more librarians commit to individual and sustained reflection and practices, more of us can serve and be served from a well of abundance and clarity, now and over time. We are growing a much-needed movement to rekindle and soothe the soul of our society. While librarians' expertise is not required, our commitment and curiosity to explore are a must.

The genesis of this book sprang from Richard's mindfulness presentation (with colleagues) at the American Library Association (ALA) Annual Conference in June 2016. Afterward, he and Madeleine created a Facebook group, Mindfulness for Librarians, with Jenny joining the project soon after. Two years later, membership has grown to more than eight hundred librarians around the world and from all types of libraries. The robust sharing has been complemented by the group's "virtual hangouts," which foster deeper discussions and forge new friendships. We even meditate together online! It became clear that the stories we were sharing deserved an even wider audience. Jamie Santoro, our wonderful editor at ALA, agreed. Our call for submissions was met with a remarkably strong response; our only regret is not being able to include all the excellent submissions.

You can read this book cover to cover or simply flip to whichever stories capture your attention. We hope the experience stirs up ideas for your own recipes for integrating mindfulness in your library. For nonlibrarians reading this book, we believe you'll find a bevy of possibilities to adapt for your own needs. Get connected with us. Join the Mindfulness for Librarians Facebook group (www.facebook.com/groups/mindfulnessforlibrarians/). Academic librarians interested in incorporating mindfulness into their teaching can also join ACRL's Contemplative Pedagogy Interest Group (www.ala.org/acrl/aboutacrl/directoryofleadership/interestgroups/acr-igcp/).

We wish you well on this unique journey—including your personal practice—as you revisit and reflect on these stories and cook up something new in your library.

PART
I

Library as Hub

1

Cultivating a "Mindful Medicine" Ethos

Rebecca Snyder and Robin O'Hanlon

In the middle of Manhattan and confronted with the disparities between privilege on the Mt. Sinai medical campus and that within the waiting rooms, Rebecca, a former doula and library technologist, and Robin, marketing director, wondered whether infusing mindfulness into innovative programming could stretch beyond exercises to create radically held space for transformational dialog in solidarity with a humanist medicine ethos. In recognition of our compatible interests, we co-organized a guided meditation workshop with our director as part of a new series she envisioned: "mindfulness for medicine." During the workshop and while debriefing afterward, we surfaced the potential missed opportunity of solely offering contemplative library programming as meditation training. The workshop was popular. As educators with adequate space, a large urban academic medical center full of expertise, and a passion for storytelling, we began to think of our new Mindful Medicine program as a museum education program and identified ourselves as "curators."

In medicine, issues of ethical concern are often labeled "medical humanities" and sandwiched between topics akin to contemplative practices such as visual literacy and creative expression. Interventional strategies to address the mental health of physicians and physicians-in-training are called "wellness," "empathy," "resilience" or, occasionally, "self-compassion." While attention is given to the neurological benefits of mindfulness as a pillar of resilience or as a component of self-care, examining relationships between mindfulness practice and the taking of ethical action is relatively new. In both respects, educators, administrators, and clinicians struggle to devote time to formation of a mindful ethos in the data-drowning, frenetic clinical environment.

As mindfulness becomes more widespread throughout our culture, many people use the label colloquially, as if everyone is in agreement about its meaning or purpose. In our story, we give attention to practices of mindfulness, like that of Linda Graham, as one of the pillars of resilience, or "bouncing back." We also emphasize its relationship to awareness by making connections between the products of mindfulness and the potential action of an aware mind.

I See Trauma and Can Develop a Response

Early in our collaboration and planning, a series of traumatic events affected our campus climate. First, a student committed suicide on campus. Less than two weeks later, the dean of our medical school became a target for work-related gun violence. During these weeks, the student presence in the library swelled to almost beyond its physical capacity. Anguish, confusion, and sorrow within our space were palpable, and student groups actively vocalized concerns about everything from mental health to social justice in our local and adjacent communities. As our medical education dean described in his 2017 *New England Journal of Medicine* article, "Kathryn," our partners in Medical Education sought to "significantly enhance mental health and well-being resources for our students." We in the library considered how we could contribute to these efforts by offering a unique chance to stimulate dialog around charged topics.

We chose to join a groundswell of reactions taking place among our students, residents, and faculty after another series of disruptive events. A prominent educator's dismissal following sexual abuse reports of patients was followed by a growing protest movement within our student and faculty communities in reaction to governmental threat aimed at our DACA students.

The focal point of our outreach programming was the development of Mindful Medicine, a series of engaging workshops focused on the humanistic emotional, ethical, and spiritual aspects of clinical practice and the patient experience. We listened to skeptical remarks and confusion from our colleagues about the relevancy of the series to library operations and whether it reflected the library's core mission. We were asked, "If this series is simply about bringing different groups and individuals together to engage in mindful discourse, how is this helping the library? If we are not leveraging the series to directly promote library services, resources, or expertise, how does it benefit us?" We were convinced, though, that this type of programming was an important form of community building, perhaps even a valve release, and would ultimately create positive associations about the library as a center for knowledge creation and contemplative practice. We wanted to move away from a purely transactional form of outreach—library "show and tell" of services has a tendency to limit our participation in activities that immediately and directly enhance usage of knowledge products or space.

The first program in the Mindful Medicine series, delivered in April 2016, was titled Narrative Medicine: A Workshop for Students and Providers. We partnered with a graduate medical educator and a physician faculty member from medical humanities. Both trained in narrative medicine, they helped us design an educational intervention in the form of a workshop to bring reflection techniques to our campus.

Where Is the Charge? What Are My Resources?

After this initial program, we formalized the program development process but intentionally left themes open to be shaped by "whatever may arise." For each installment, we would first "listen" to the news: institutional newsletters, student groups, our partners, and academic medicine publications. Influenced by student concerns or emerging issues in medicine and medical education, we would focus on a theme. It was our desire to mirror current medical education initiatives and research activities already taking place within our community. However, we first had to acknowledge ourselves as culture observers and confront our biases. Then we needed to allow ourselves to address curricular gaps or topics that seemed to carry a notable charge, warranting more psychic space than we believed the classroom would provide. It was, to say the least, painful and scary, particularly in November 2016 America.

Nevertheless, we were spurred on by gratitude and feedback from participants who wanted to engage in contemplative learning in a more informal, interactive space than is offered in a classroom or a Grand Rounds presentation.

Once the theme was imagined, we would identify potential facilitators to participate in the program. These speakers, educators, activists, and community members were primarily recruited from our home institution based on our knowledge of their work or reputation. We frequently leveraged our collaborators' networks for recommendations, whether from in-house or from another institution. We met with the team to discuss the approach, chose target audiences, and created the learning objectives that were most appropriate. Format types combined in each session included brief presentations, panel discussions, case-based/problem-solving discussions, small group discussions, and hands-on practice workshops.

After the first program, we had enough documentation to seek continuing medical education credit for participants in the series. In September 2016, the Mindful Medicine series was accredited through our institution's postgraduate school for up to two American Medical Association Physician's Recognition Award Category 1 credits for participants, which incentivized attendance and demonstrated the value of the series' content to key stakeholders. The Continuing Medical Education (CME) application was extensive and required that we identify specific clinical gaps that our programming would work to fill. The application also required the identification of specific learning outcomes/objectives, target audiences, tools/strategies to reinforce learning results, professional competencies (i.e., patient-centered care, interdisciplinary and communication skills, performance in practice), and patient safety considerations.

Options to Change Perspective Are Available to Me

By the time our November 2016 program went live, we were actively integrating our contemplative approach with critical pedagogy and social justice librarianship. We reached out to Mount Sinai's Center for Transgender Medicine and Surgery, which then actualized Turn Up the Mic: Reflections on Experiences with Transgender Medicine, a storytelling event with the central theme of "amplification of the patient voice." In this program, a panel of individuals who had undergone gender reassignment surgery discussed perspectives on their care, including the conflicted nuances of communicating with providers. The ensuing discussion was sensitively moderated by Barbara Warren, PsyD, director for LGBT Programs and Policies in the Mount Sinai Office for Diversity and Inclusion and local activist for NYC trans communities. Offering the microphone to patients to tell their stories, their voices were literally amplified. Their stories also allowed the clinicians and medical students in the room to mindfully reflect on their own current or future practice, consider shared decision-making with their patients, and engage with the patients to learn more about their experiences.

Due to the sensitive nature of the topics explored and the intention to create a boundary between participants and the "presence" of academic medicine hierarchy in the space, we selected experienced educators and interactive methods for the program. Beneficial relationships with our social work and spiritual care communities ensured mindful in-room engagement between participants and influenced the themes and content developed going forward. As the program and our relationships with staff from the medical school and health system matured, we were able to approach increasingly complex topics like spiritual dimensions of LBGTQQ geriatric care and trauma in health care.

This May Be Rhizomatic Rather Than Mechanical

Typically, in library literature, we report on "what we did" and how it could be a blueprint for actualizing a similar project or program. In the spirit of contemplative practice, though, designing an intervention or experience can be more of an art than a replicable scientific process. Like bricolage, we made choices somewhat intuitively and with materials not traditionally central to a librarian praxis. Translating this program to our new institutions would require significant transformation and, in the end, would likely look nothing like the original.

However, mindful awareness can radically influence our experiments with pedagogy by disrupting the default professional scripts or biases in one's head that may arise when considering how, or even whether, to design an intervention. As educators, we may be situated between potential connections while possessing insight or resources to make them happen. Sometimes, we don't see them. Other times, we may be underresourced internally or environmentally and thus unable to act. Occasionally, awareness, collectivity, and privilege may align and an opportunity comes to fruition. Envisioning our institutional repository as an ethics human library was bold for a couple of library educators in a large academic medical center. Yet as we pitched the connection between mindfulness and the potential for improved awareness in clinical decision-making and patient care, we discovered that our institution had ample resources and a community ready to gather. The initial idea may, on the surface, have arisen from environmental scanning, but the manifestation and evolution of the program came from seeing beyond strategic opportunities and threats to the heart of the matter. Our community members wanted to be connected.

In the end, we were rewarded many times over with gratitude from participants and the proliferation of a community. But in sharing the experience, its nature as a watery memory, a blip, reveals itself. Equanimity needed to acknowledge continued suffering within our medical education communities while also celebrating this story remains difficult. Mindful reflection is essential to stabilize our state of being, manage our own states of overwhelm, and avoid reverting to numbness or "business as usual." The reconciliation of our limitations as librarians is itself a target of our contemplative practice now as we ground, resource, and move forward.

2

Accidentally Sustainable

Building a Weekly Meditation
Community

Laura Horwood-Benton

Part of the responsibility of a programming librarian is identifying and collaborating with local enti-
ties for the benefit of the entire community. Nowhere
has this been more evident in my career than in Portsmouth
Public Library's long-running Weekly Meditation program. Our
region has an abundance of yoga studios, Buddhist groups, and
mental health practitioners and a community desperate for
mindfulness instruction. The key to our program's success was
bringing these populations together.

"A Wonderful Gift in the Midst of so Much That Clutters the Mind, Hearts"

So wrote one patron on our feedback form about
attending Weekly Meditation at the library. These words are not
unfamiliar—we have heard them so many times with regard to
the library as a whole. The public library is a refuge for many, a
place to be still, a place to practice both mindfulness and compassion. Offering a formal, facilitated meditation on a weekly
basis seems to my colleagues and me just an extension of this
mission. We began this endeavor with high hopes—but still
never expecting it to last for three years and counting!

Setting the Stage

The demand for a weekly sit was made evident by the sign-ups for several multiweek mindfulness courses offered at the library in 2013 and 2014. Each time we offered the course, we were overbooked with a long waiting list. We also heard from attendees that they were looking for ways to continue their meditation practice. We began to explore the possibility of offering this weekly meet-up, tapping the connections we knew who might be interested in volunteering. Once we had the beginning of a program, we announced it at the end of the mindfulness course, engaging a ready-made audience.

Weekly Meditation

The program is made possible by the generosity of a roster of five to eight volunteer practitioners, each who leads a different style of practice, including mindfulness, loving compassion, Zen, and yogic meditations, plus body-based practices and contemplative singing. We host two forty-five-minute sessions per week:

Mondays, 6:00–6:45 p.m.

Wednesdays, 12:15–1:00 p.m.

While our lineup has shifted over the past three years, we maintain a core group of volunteers. These include

Cathy, a circulation staff member who leads contemplative singing (Cathy is our only paid teacher, as she leads her sessions "on the clock");

Candradasa, an ordained Buddhist who also happens to be my husband (bless those library spouses!);

Suzanne, our deputy city attorney who has been leading a weekly sit at city hall for years;

Avi, a local teacher who belongs to the Linji meditation school and has been a student of Zen master Thich Nhat Hanh for more than two decades; and

Liz, a practitioner who previously led several multi-week mindfulness courses at the library.

We have also had a variety of yoga and mental health practitioners as facilitators. Each volunteer is invited to bring handouts, cards, or other materials to promote his or her own business, community, or other events.

Other Details

- Each volunteer leads one to three sessions per month, depending on availability.
- Schedules are drafted and approved each year in three segments: January–April, May–August, and September–December.
- The program is run by two staff members, with occasional setup assistance by one or two others, as required by scheduling.
- Setup requires less than fifteen minutes. A library staff member puts up signs, assembles chairs, sets out meditation cushions and handouts with the schedule and teacher bios, and displays publicity materials if provided by teachers.
- On average, we see around ten to fifteen people each session, sometimes growing to more than twenty.

What Worked

Session Timing

We chose these times based on input from teachers, staff scheduling, and (most importantly) the goal of maximizing attendance. Attendees may be able to slip away on their Wednesday lunch break or stop by for a quick predinner Monday session. We hoped the range of options would accommodate many people's schedules: parents, full-time workers, and retired folks, among others. Attendance and feedback have shown that we were correct.

We had many discussions about the length of sessions, as forty-five minutes can feel short when you factor in introductions and questions. Indeed, some bumps occurred with scheduling, as people often feel the need to stay afterward to speak one-on-one with the teacher. And yet, as one of our teachers put it, "somehow less than an hour seems more manageable to people, especially beginners. . . . For me, the whole point of this project is accessibility." We have also found that forty-five minutes is easier to slot in between programs.

Attracting Beginners

The program was intended for beginners, and we have found that on average, around 40 percent of attendees are new to meditation. As one wrote, it is a "great chance to explore different forms of meditation!" Attendance has remained generally constant since the beginning of the program, and this does not show signs of changing. With a population of more than twenty thousand in Portsmouth alone, we think it will be quite some time before everyone in our community has learned to meditate!

Volunteer Investment

We are pleasantly surprised anew with each passing season at the level of investment and ownership our volunteer practitioners feel in the program. Our core group has participated from the beginning, and their interest has not waned. We check in with them each time we create a new schedule regarding both their desired level of involvement and any suggestions for improvements, and I believe this care creates a collaborative environment that strengthens their investment.

What We Learned

Publishing Our Schedule

From the beginning, we included information about each teacher in our advertising, so participants knew what they could expect when they attended. We were wary at first of publishing the schedule of volunteers, as we anticipated teachers might switch or cancel at the last minute. We also worried that attendees might choose a "favorite" teacher and only attend those sessions, to the detriment of the program's integrity. However, we received so many requests for a schedule that we eventually shared it, online and in print. We found that there were fewer swaps than expected and that attendance remained generally consistent, although some favoritism of teachers does occur. Overall, people feel more agency and comfort when they can choose which style of meditation to learn.

Sangha

In Pali and Sanskrit, the word *sangha* means "community." Buddhists use this term to describe their spiritual community. Whether ordained or lay practitioners, all practice together in friendship and support and in a way that is ongoing and uplifting. Apart from the longevity of our Weekly Meditation program, the thing that has surprised us the most is the library *sangha*.

We anticipated that people might attend for a while to learn to meditate and eventually move on to another context. We expected that those who wished to go deeper would connect with particular teachers and perhaps begin attending their events/sits/communities. In fact, we used this as a selling point with prospective volunteer leaders, offering that they might in fact "drum up business" in this way. But people move on far less often than we expected! Rather, the library seems to have formed a community of its own, with an interfaith/secular foundation. About 60 percent of attendees at any given session are "regulars" who come each week or even twice a week, who have begun to connect with each other, and who see the library as their main community of practice. Other programming librarians may recognize this as one of the most rewarding experiences in our profession: witnessing community being created before our eyes because of our actions! We feel honored to be helping this *sangha* thrive.

Looking to the Future

Our focus for the program at the present moment is identifying at least one additional teacher, for more comfort and flexibility of scheduling. Beyond that, our group has a few ideas and wishes for the future:

- more in-depth feedback forms to hear from our regular attendees
- yearly teacher meet-ups (with pizza!) to discuss the program
- a onetime meditation "fair" or "open house" for new people to meet all the teachers at once
- quarterly or monthly weekend sessions
- events specifically for children and teens

Bringing Weekly Meditation to Your Library

Will Weekly Meditation thrive at your library? We believe these are the key replicable elements of our program:

Critical Mass of Instructors: Can you kick off a weekly session with participation from at least four or five local instructors? Bonus if they are library staff, existing volunteers, or have other strong ties to your library.

Community Interest: Has your community shown an interest in mindfulness, either at your library or elsewhere in your community? Does your region have at least one or two yoga studios? Have people asked for such a program?

Time to Grow: Does your staff have time to maintain the program for at least six months to monitor growth and build up an audience and a following?

Nonattachment: At the same time, can you make peace with the fact that this program may have a fixed life span? We know that all things are impermanent! So too is each library program and service. Cultivate your own flexibility as you plan.

Connection to Your Volunteers: Does your staff have the time and interest to maintain a connection with your volunteer teachers? Can you begin from a place of harmonious collaboration?

3

The Be Project

Sparking a Quiet Revolution in Rural Kentucky

Katie Scherrer

A few years ago a team of five educators from both within and outside of a school system in rural Kentucky wondered what could happen if teachers and students received information about, exposure to, and practice in mindfulness as part of their school day. The result was the Be Project, a locally developed mindfulness education curriculum for teachers and students in the Clark County Public Schools in rural Kentucky. Together, this team obtained funding, developed a curriculum, trained teachers, and supported them after the training both in person and online. Model classrooms at every school in the county received follow-up, one-on-one sessions with the project leaders, assisting with the cultivation of the teachers' own mindfulness practices as well as the instruction of mindfulness in the classroom for students in Pre-K through twelfth grade. Responding to the high rates of poverty, addiction, and other family struggles prevalent in the community, the project utilized a trauma-informed universal design. The Be Project has now taken on its own life, sparking a "quiet revolution" of a more mindful culture in various spaces throughout the county.

The Idea

The Be Project began with Kara Davies, who was working at the time as a high school guidance counselor and pursuing her EdD. As is the case for many of us, events in Kara's personal life led her to discover the practice of mindfulness. It wasn't long before that practice started to show up in her interactions with students. She could feel herself in tense interactions experiencing that little pause between action and reaction where she was able to ask the question, "What is best for this student or group of students *in this moment*?" Seeing how effectively this change helped her navigate her many responsibilities, she began to feel called to share these principles with teachers, students, and the community. However, Kara knew what she was envisioning was too much to tackle on her own, so she began reaching out to local mindfulness experts and building what would eventually become the Be Project team.

The Team

Kara first reached out to Allison Nelson, a trusted colleague and school psychologist with a personal mindfulness practice. Allison had been noticing similar changes in her professional life as her mindfulness practice was developing and had been wondering many of the same questions as Kara regarding how a district-wide adoption of mindfulness—both in and out of the classroom—could empower educators and improve school climates. Both being newer to practicing mindfulness themselves, they sought the input of other local wellness professionals.

Erin Smith is a yoga teacher and teacher trainer who owns a local yoga studio, The Om Place, and online companion resource, The Om Channel. Erin worked in the local school system as a school librarian for many years and is a well-known and deeply trusted community leader.

Cindy Reed is a licensed clinical social worker, a yoga teacher, and a certified Daring Way™ facilitator who has trained with Brené Brown. Cindy became exposed to mindfulness while studying Dialectical Behavior Therapy in the late 1990s. Cindy has considerable expertise in the impact of trauma and the utilization of trauma-informed universal design.

As the team initially began collaborating, they quickly realized that though they all had the skills to share mindfulness with teachers and students at the intermediate through high school levels, they were lacking expertise in adapting mindfulness practices for the very young. Katie Scherrer, a children's yoga and mindfulness teacher and former children's librarian, was brought on board to fill this gap.

Funding

With the team in place, it was time to find a way to fund the project for its initial development and pilot implementation. A logical place to begin was with the Greater Clark Foundation, whose mission "is to make Clark County, Kentucky, one of the best places in the country to live, work and play." One strategy the Greater Clark Foundation undertakes to execute its mission is the distribution of small-scale *What's Your Ambition?!* grants, designed to create "bright spots" within the community: actions taken to creatively respond to community challenges and improve overall quality of life. The Be Project team worked together under Kara's leadership to secure the initial ten-thousand-dollar *What's Your Ambition?!* grant used to develop a cohesive mindfulness curriculum for pre-K through twelfth grade and to provide a first round of training to staff primarily located at the high school and junior high. A second grant of the same amount funded the pilot implementation of the project.

Implementation

Implementation of the Be Project began with professional development workshops for more than one hundred district employees, including principals, teachers, mental health professionals, and support staff. In these three-hour workshops, participants learned what mindfulness is and were exposed to neuroscience research that elucidates the positive changes that mindfulness practice can have on the brain (particularly in the areas of reduced stress response and neuroplasticity). They also learned about ways trauma can change brain functioning and how to use trauma-informed universal design to present mindfulness practices in their classrooms in ways that minimize the risk of triggering those students who have been impacted by trauma. Katie, Erin, and Cindy made frequent visits to model classrooms identified in each school, where they demonstrated the use of the curriculum with students and supported teachers and guidance counselors in the development of their personal mindfulness practice. Online support was also provided to the model classroom teachers, including regular e-mail contact, video demonstrations and guided practices, and an electronic discussion list for the teachers to share their experiences. The entire implementation process lasted about three months.

Results

Though the Be Project team members all have ample experience practicing and teaching mindfulness, they have less expertise in the area of rigorous research design. Thus results of the pilot phase of the Be Project are mostly anecdotal. However, the observable changes we can report are encouraging. For example, students at the high school have created their own Be Club, which a teacher mentor oversees, providing weekly space in the school for the students to engage in their own mindfulness practices and occasionally receive instruction from local mindfulness practitioners in the community. Examples of positive change are not limited to older students; preschool teacher Kamerin Hall recounts this example of the impact of the Be Project in her class:

> One of the children in my classroom has a developmental delay in the area of social emotional skills. At the beginning of the school year, she would cry if she didn't get her way or was upset for any reason. Katie used a "breathing ball" to show the children how to take a deep breath and make the ball bigger and as you exhale the ball gets smaller. After teaching this lesson multiple times and talking with the child about how to control her "strong" feelings, I began to see a major change in her emotional health. One day, she was in the kitchen area and wanted to play with a certain doll. Someone else was playing with that doll; she began to get upset. She realized she was getting mad and walked over to the carpet area and got the breathing ball. She stood on the carpet and took three deep

breaths, and then she returned to her center to continue playing. It was such a magical moment that I began to cry.

Perhaps the greatest testament to the value of this initiative is the commitment of the school system to continue funding it in order to implement it district-wide as a component of social-emotional learning. Training for all principals and assistant principals took place at the close of the 2017–18 school year, with training for all staff at each school to follow during the 2018–19 school year. Depending on funding available, plans are being crafted to potentially expand and increase the in-school support for the educators with the ultimate goal of identifying the district leaders who will continue the work of the Be Project independent of the support of the original team.

Ripples in the Community

The work of the Be Project has spread to other community organizations outside of the school system, which are also now developing strategies for using mindfulness with their staff and clientele. One example is the Mountain Comprehensive Care Center (MCCC), a mental health organization that provides multiple services to the community, including an after-school program for young people who have been identified as struggling with moderate to severe mental health disorders (examples include severe ADHD, anxiety disorders, and PTSD). After learning about the Be Project and seeing some of its impact on teachers and students, the MCCC reached out to team members Cindy Reed and Katie Scherrer to provide staff training to their social workers on trauma-informed design and the adaptation of mindfulness practices for children. The training was so effective that MCCC decided to look for a way to expand the practices to others serving children and families in the community. As of this writing, they are applying for grant funds that will allow them to provide mindfulness training free of charge to up to eighty community members from various agencies, including the library, parks and recreation, early childhood education centers, faith-based organizations, and more.

Lessons for Libraries

Collaborate with local subject matter experts. Perhaps your staff lacks a person who is steeped enough in practicing mindfulness to competently teach others. That's fine. There are others in your community with the skillset who would love to fill that role. Whether you are interested in offering programs for the community or using mindfulness internally with staff, look for local mindfulness teachers who you could hire as an outside expert to help you get started.

We must practice what we teach. If we want to share the reduced stress response and increased clarity that mindfulness has to offer with others, we must first develop our own practice. We cannot think our way into receiving the benefits of mindfulness.

Be connected within your community. With most things in life, it is easy to find ourselves on autopilot in our jobs, doing what we've always done because that's the way we've always done it. We may have an opinion about what our community does or does not want from us based on something we tried years ago, or we may believe stories about other organizations in our community based on how relationships have unfolded in the past or something we've heard third hand. No need to feel guilty or judge yourself if this rings true; it happens. But now might be a good time to cultivate "beginners' mind" and see your community with fresh eyes, perhaps imagining you're starting your job over from square one. What's happening in your community to support the mental health and well-being of all residents? Who are some of the key leaders serving your community that you can reach out to in order to learn more about how they are supporting the same folks you serve within your own mission? One of the most exciting aspects of the Be Project is that though it began within a school system, it is spreading beyond its initial audience to include multiple stakeholders invested in the vision of providing tomorrow's leaders the tools they need to thrive. That's the quiet shift of a culture change—a true revolution.

4

Providing a Space to Rest

Weaving Restorative Yoga into the Strategic Plan

Millie Jackson

The ability to quiet the mind and take a short time to pause and rest is essential for health and well-being. Lack of rest is well documented in our current society, and in the assessment-driven academic community, it is particularly prevalent. Sleep deprivation is caused by a number of factors but impacts memory, attention, learning, and mood. Some studies have suggested that up to 50 percent of college students are sleep deprived. Adults are equally sleep deprived and in need of time to pause and recharge. When the University of Alabama released its strategic plan in 2016 and subsequently requested that the colleges and units on campus create plans of their own based on it, I saw an opportunity for the University Libraries to include a better-defined program to support mindfulness and rest through restorative yoga sessions. Both the university's strategic plan and the University Libraries' included goals to support work-life balance. These new goals extended the work that was already under way on campus. WellBAMA, the employee wellness program, was already established on campus. Mindfulness meditation; YogaFit; Sleep More, Stress Less; and other programs focused on slowing down were available for faculty and staff, as were equivalent programs addressing all of these issues for students through Health Promotion and Wellness.

The question I asked myself and others was, What could the University Libraries add to these existing programs that could perhaps fill a niche that was not being addressed elsewhere on campus?

I had already led classes in gentle yoga in the University Libraries and for programs across campus, which had initiated collaboration between the University Libraries and the Well-BAMA program to use rooms in two of our buildings for the on-going yoga classes. The gentle yoga classes were superseded by YogaFit-based classes, however, and the locations changed over the years to make classes accessible in different areas across campus. Ongoing meditation groups also existed. Most of those groups focused on sitting meditation and met regularly in the student center or in dorms. One of our science librarians has been a longtime promoter and organizer of programs featuring yoga and mind-body connections. In 2015, this librarian, along with one of our instruction librarians, organized a multiday Mindfulness for the Academic workshop with Dr. Vasundhara Doraswamy, which featured the benefits of meditation, yoga, and mindfulness in the classroom. In June 2016, the library sponsored International Yoga Day events, including several classes and films about yoga. Up until the summer of 2017, the programs offered were generally collaborations with other units on campus or were special events, but there was an interest in offering a more consistent and ongoing program.

Restorative Yoga

After some discussion and assessment of programs already available around campus, I determined that Restorative Yoga would be a beneficial program. At the time I proposed it, I had recently completed a two-hundred-hour yoga teacher train-ing course as well as a fifty-hour certification in Restorative Yoga, a deeply nourishing and quiet practice that I felt was im-portant to offer. There are few classes in this style of yoga offered in the Tuscaloosa area, and the classes that had been offered through the campus recreation center had ceased because the teacher moved on.

Restorative Yoga allows for rest and relaxation through sup-ported poses. Props such as blankets and blocks allow for total relaxation of the body. Poses allow for spine movement in different ways to increase well-being, and inverted poses, as simple as legs up the wall, reverse the effects of gravity for improved blood flow in the body. Numerous medical and scientific studies over the past few decades document the benefits of Restorative Yoga as a practice. Scholars such as Dr. Herbert Benson and his team of researchers at the Benson-Henry Institute at Harvard and long-time teachers like Judith Hanson Lasater and Jillian Pransky have provided studies to support the benefits of Restorative Yoga practices. Taking as little as twenty minutes to stop and quiet the mind and body can be beneficial to overall health and well-being.

I received approval to purchase twenty blankets and twenty yoga blocks to begin the program. Participants were asked to provide their own yoga mat, though I had a few that I brought and provided as needed. Part of my training was in the use of minimal props, so I knew that a few blankets and a block for each participant would be sufficient to teach successful classes. The program was piloted in summer 2017 with a few classes offered in July and August. Since it was summer, there were not as many people on campus, but I started seeing a consistent group attending the classes when they were offered. I continued into the fall with classes provided for an eight-week period and longer sessions after work and on Sunday afternoons. The main issue that I had in the fall was that I had been unable to book a consistent day and time for the class. The room I was using is one of the most popular meeting spaces on campus because of its size and location. Longer sessions did not have a very large turnout, although the participants who did come enjoyed them and appreciated their length; scheduling conflicts with other events during the week and sports on the weekends impacted attendance. For the spring and fall semesters of 2018, I scheduled the room well ahead of time so that I would have the same day and time on the calendar. I did not require reservations for the class because I did not want to prevent people from attending at the last minute. This turned into a problem when I was sick one week in February and did not have a contact list, and unfortunately, the entire series was marked as canceled instead of just one day. It took a few weeks to build up attendance again, and I began collecting names and e-mail addresses in the event that anything else happened.

In a thirty-minute class, there is not enough time for many poses—only two to three per class with a short warm-up—but there is enough to allow for relaxation. I watch the class and determine when to have them move to another pose based on comfort in the current pose. I also play music. My style of teaching is not to talk much but to let students have time to sink in and relax. At first, many of the attendees were new to Restorative Yoga and did not expect a class where they would essentially "do nothing" for thirty minutes, but the class has since drawn a core group as well as drop-ins. Students come in a bit skeptical but frequently return, especially graduate students who are looking for ways to deal with the stress of classes, work, and/or teaching. One challenge I have faced has been working with a few participants who were pregnant. I did not have much experience and had to consult with some fellow teachers. I also brought props from home for these students and created a special sequence for them based on how far into their pregnancies they were.

Reflections

Going forward, I will continue to seek a schedule with specific days and times. My plan is to offer an eight-week series each semester and to incorporate the labyrinth, a program that is just being developed at the university, with Restorative Yoga for longer sessions. Marketing and promoting the classes continues to be necessary to make it sustainable as a program. To this end, the public relations person for the library created a poster for me that remained in the lobby during the semester, and the classes were also added to the campus calendar and listed in the wellness newsletter. I reached out to faculty who teach graduate students and asked them to promote the classes to their students as well.

Through the offering of Restorative Yoga, the library is becoming a place that nurtures not only the mind but also the body and spirit. Restorative Yoga offers a space for relaxation and relief from stress and tension. The classes have been well received so far. Developing more programs that integrate mindfulness practices that aid people in "letting go" of the busyness of life is an ongoing goal. Programs that encourage conscious relaxation support the strategic plans but also, more importantly, lifelong health and well-being.

PART II

Innovative Services

5

Mindful McQuade

Mindfulness in the Heart of a Small College Campus

Catherine Wong, Katherine LaFlamme, and Michaela Keating

Mindfulness-based programs such as yoga, meditation, and therapy pets are popular ways to reduce stress and appear regularly on college campuses. While the McQuade Library, the heart and hub of activities at Merrimack College, made minor attempts to provide such programs, there was a clear need for more effort. With the development of Mindful McQuade—a collaborative effort of librarians, faculty, and health counselors from across the campus community—students now have access to resources for improved health and productivity. This initiative offers the additions of exercise bicycles, a meditation room, classes taught by professionals in mindfulness-based stress reduction (MBSR) and breath work, mindfulness books, games, and kits with materials for check out, and houseplants to borrow long term for residence halls. Through Mindful McQuade, the library provides a holistic approach to addressing students' needs and aims to develop their mental, physical, and spiritual well-being.

Hamel Health Partnership

As a twenty-four-hour campus center and popular study spot, McQuade Library is a hub of productive activity as well as high stress. To align the Mindful McQuade initiative with

other student wellness programs on campus, McQuade librarians leveraged their existing relationship with Hamel Health and
Counseling Center (HHCC), the college's health and wellness office.
The Center emphasizes mindfulness as a part of well-being, providing students with the education needed to make wise choices
for both physical and mental health. Beginning five years ago,
this collaboration started when McQuade and the HHCC began
to offer therapy pet visits and chair massage to students during
the high-stress final exam period. While these two activities
remain among the most popular and beloved campus events,
this partnership has evolved further. McQuade's access services
and technical services teams have since offered use of the circulation software Evergreen to assist the Center with loaning materials for well-being. Starting in fall 2017, Vitamin D lamps
purchased by the HHCC joined the materials on the library's
course reserves shelves to help students combat the symptoms
of Seasonal Affective Disorder.

The HHCC's emphasis on mindful self-care and wellness education made including the Center in the new Mindful McQuade
initiative a natural fit. With the Center's trained staff teaching
MBSR workshops in the library meditation space (repurposed
offices), we now have a low-cost way to provide high-quality,
weekly meditation programs. This increases the visibility of the
Center's services by providing them a neutral setting, with the
added benefit of introducing students to the new meditation
space. When library staff began looking to partner with other
campus departments, doing a quick scan to see who else was
offering mindfulness-related programming provided information
about whom to contact and where to focus the library's efforts to
ensure a united approach to a mindful campus.

Meditation Space and Mindful Programming

Creating a physical space where students could shut
out the world and tune into their inner guru as well as attend
classes was important to the success of the program. The question was where to carve out this space in a building already
threatening to burst. Finding a quiet space with a door was a
challenge, but as the saying goes, one person's trash is another
person's treasure. A lower level library seminar room that was

utilized as a faculty office had previously been vacated due to limited HVAC availability, and although it was filled with desks and filing cabinets, it did have a carpeted floor and a functioning door. Once the unwanted furniture was removed and the carpet was cleaned, this twelve-by-twenty-eight-foot room turned out to be a perfect spot for a meditation space. Though chilly, space heaters are available for when the room is in use. The Provost Innovation Grant allowed the library to purchase twelve sets of meditation mats and pillows, yoga mats, and blankets, as well as a salt lamp and twinkle lights. Repurposing and upcycling items found around the library yielded a small table, cubbies, and office plants, which completed the meditation room setup. People are asked to remove their shoes before entering the room. A CD player along with meditation CDs are available for visitors to use, as well as mindful books and magazines. The room is left unlocked so students can drop in between classes to turn on the twinkle lights and a CD or to just simply relax.

Once the meditation room was ready, two classes a week were offered in the space. On Thursday afternoons, Jim Howland, EdD, a licensed independent clinical social worker from the HHCC, offered a four-week course called Stress Reduction and Mindfulness. In this mini MBSR course, Dr. Howland also provided students with podcasts to practice the techniques they learned in class while at home. On Thursday mornings, McQuade offered a course entitled Empowered Breathing and Meditation for Anxiety and Stress Reduction using funds from the Provost Innovation Grant. This eight-week course was taught by Danielle Federico, a professional life coach, certified yoga instructor, and breath work facilitator. With years of experience, excellent teaching styles, and calm demeanors, both instructors brought breathing techniques, strategies to deal with stress and anxiety, and gentle yogic movement to the library. Students as well as faculty and staff flocked to the classes, filling the room for most of the sessions.

Kits

To promote mindfulness both inside and outside of the library, nine Mindful McQuade Kits were developed, any of which can be checked out by the Merrimack community for a two-week period with one renewal. Each of the kits focuses on a different aspect of mindfulness, exposing the patron to various relaxation practices. The themes presented in the kits include bird-watching, balancing chakra, meditation, gardening, sound healing, creative healing, and yoga. There are three bird-watching kits available, which include a set of binoculars, a Sibley field guide, and a laminated pamphlet of birds in Massachusetts. In the chakra kit, you'll find several stones and crystals, chakra flags, a stress ball, an introductory book, and two chakra music CDs, while in the meditation kit you'll find a sound machine, Baoding balls, a finger labyrinth, a book on meditation, and four meditation CDs. The gardening kit is made up of small tools such as a trowel, pruners, a cultivator, and a transplanter, as well as gloves, a book on gardening, and three nature-themed music CDs. The sound healing kit includes a small singing bowl with its base, a rain stick, an energy chime (handmade in America), a stress ball, three sound healing music CDs, and two books (one pertaining to sound healing and one as an introduction to using the singing bowl). In the creative healing kit, you'll find a zen water-drawing board, colored pencils, a coloring book, affirmation cards, a stress ball, and two music CDs. Lastly, the yoga kit includes a mat, a yoga brick and strap, three yoga music CDs, and Christina Brown's *The Yoga Bible*. All of the kits (aside from the yoga kit, which has its own special bag to hold the mat) are contained in clear, plastic over-the-shoulder bags, making it easy for the patron to see the materials inside. Also in the bags is a contents list, so both the patron and library staff can keep track of the items in each kit. The goal of the Mindful McQuade Kits is to encourage people to try different mindfulness practices that they may not otherwise have the chance to experience. We really want to stress that mindfulness is accessible to everyone and that there is no set stereotype when it comes to your health and well-being.

Plants

If you love your spider plant it will love you back and bless you with many new spider plants, but what to do with all those little ones? Research Center librarians started potting them up and handing them out to anyone who wanted one for their residence hall, office, or home. Houseplants help purify the air and give college students something to take care of and love. The program started when a student from out of state asked the librarians to look after her plant over the summer break after she saw all the plants in the Research Center. Another student brought in a dead plant and asked librarians to perform a miracle. When a miracle was not possible, a substitute plant was sent home with the student. Before too long, plants were being "loaned" from the library with no expectation of return. In order to save money and the environment, plants were potted in extra mugs that staff members brought from home. Kitchen cabinets were cleared out and mugs were repurposed, making this a fairly low-cost but high-impact program. Students were thrilled with their plants and often returned to the Research Center to give librarians an update on the health of their precious little ones.

Bikes in the Library

In collaboration with Dr. April Bowling, a professor from the School of Health Sciences, the library purchased four exercise bicycles and placed them on the first and second floors

Bicycles in the Library

of the library. Purchased with funds from a Provost Innovation Grant, the bicycles allow students to take a convenient, quick, and mindful exercise break, as physical activity primes the brain for study. One pair is made up of Expresso bikes, which offer full-immersive technology so riders can navigate through various terrains or play games designed to help them ride longer. The other pair has desks attached so students can use their own devices while riding. The bikes are quiet enough for library use and signs with ideas for mindfulness are near and on the bikes. When shopping for exercise bikes, Dr. Bowling suggests procuring those with adjustable tension and a 350-pound weight limit to accommodate differing body types.

Promotion and New Partnerships

All these initiatives were not started on the same day so there was a building of momentum and word of mouth that helped with promotion. The best way to promote the meditation space was to show it to anyone who was interested. They felt instantly calm and wanted to return. A sandwich board was purchased to point toward the meditation space and promote the programs. Additionally, the *Provost's Briefing*, a weekly campus e-mail of news and events, was a big help in getting the word out about Mindful McQuade. However, after much trial and error, we realized the most strategic spot to place signage regarding library programming and events is the bathroom stalls. We printed mindful educational pages with ideas on how to take breaks from electronics and how to mindfully breathe and naturally placed advertising about Mindful McQuade near the posters. Beyond that, traditional means of promotion were utilized such as McQuade's social media accounts, the library newsletter, posters around campus, LibGuides, announcements before instructional sessions, and posts on monitors on campus.

In addition to partnering with the HHCC, the buzz on campus about Mindful McQuade helped forge a new partnership with the Office of Wellness Education (OWE). During the week before finals, the OWE offers a popular program titled Destress Fest, which includes playful activities to reduce stress such as a ball pit and Bubble Wrap popping as well as hot water and a variety of teas. Librarians took part this year by offering hula-hooping lessons, markers and coloring pages, and plant adoption, as well as showcasing the new mindfulness and bird-watching kits. The OWE is helping promote the Mindful McQuade programming via their social media and other outlets as well.

Bringing It All Together to Create a Healthier Campus

Mental and physical health awareness is a critical topic in college health centers, faculty development trainings, and student programming, and their importance in those areas cannot be understated. Bringing Mindful McQuade initiatives into the heart of campus makes these changes visible in the course of everyday life at college and normalizes the need to take a mindful moment during a busy day. Along the way, we collaborated with colleagues from across the campus community, as everyone on campus is interested in ensuring that students have healthy ways to reduce the stress that is so common to the college experience. Not only are calm and happy students better for

Coloring Mindfully

retention; they are also more successful in their academic and personal growth.

Resources for Mindfulness

6

Mindfulness Experiences

The Library Brain Booth

Katia G. Karadjova

Scholarly literature supports mindful practices, such as intentional brain breaks, emotional self-regulation, and singular focus, to help students improve study skills and knowledge retention. These practices were introduced to students in the library at Humboldt State University (HSU) about two and a half years ago when a former colleague and I started the Brain Booth (BB) Initiative, an innovative project promoting mindfulness and contemplative pedagogy. The Library Brain Booth (http://libguides.humboldt.edu/brain booth/) is an informal, experiential space to learn about the mind-body connection and optimize learning.

The mission of the Library BB reads:

> The Library Brain Booth seeks to introduce the campus community to international scientific research on the effects of mindfulness, attention, and contemplation through hands-on tools and activities in an informal, experiential setting. Students are especially encouraged to explore the positive impacts that taking an intentional brain break can have on their academic success. Although the Library Brain Booth recognizes the contributions of people of all faiths and backgrounds to mindfulness practices, it has no religious affiliation. People of all abilities, cultures, and faiths are welcome in the Library Brain Booth.

The Brain Booth has the goal of introducing mindfulness as a means of introducing students to metacognition for academic success. We use three basic tenets of mindfulness or contemplation practices to help us accomplish that:

Intentional Brain Breaks: Reminding the campus community that taking as little as two minutes to give the brain a break from thinking can lead to better focus and optimize learning.

Emotional Self-Regulation: We ask students to engage in courageous conversations both in and outside of the classroom. Teaching reflection and mindfulness is a way to prepare students to engage more successfully in those conversations while also teaching them to cultivate patience and compassion for diverse viewpoints. All of the above facilitate and complement applying critical pedagogy in the classroom as well.

Singular Thoughtful Focus: Many of our students struggle with attempting to multitask as well as fostering strong, singular focus when it is needed for short or sustained periods of time. Mindfulness training has immediate impacts on attention and focus.

As Brain Booth cofounder Marissa Mourer says, whether you call it contemplation, focus, or meditation, giving yourself an intentional space and time where you stop thinking makes you think better. That is better for physical wellness, better for emotional health, and better for intellectual growth.

At the time we started the Brain Booth, some libraries were already implementing meditation activities within their offerings. We were interested in taking it further than just meditation activities. With the financial support of two small grants from the HSU Sponsored Programs Foundation, we purchased portable biofeedback machines, sound machines, therapy lights, two pedaling fit-desks, virtual reality goggles, two Chromebooks (to run meditation videos), and coloring supplies. Through donations, we also received an old stereo to listen to meditation CDs on. The Brain Booth started offering different activity stations: Color-Relax, Light-Relax, Sound-Relax, Audio-Meditate, Prompt-Meditate, Video-Meditate, Gratitude-Express, Virtual Reality–Immerse, and Biofeedback. The biofeedback unit is a resilience-training device that measures your coherence levels and heart rate variability. Coherence directly impacts how a person physiologically reacts to and reduces stress. During the semester, we were setting up the stations in a library room twice a week for two hours each, staffing the Brain Booth ourselves.

"There is a sanctuary on the second floor of the HSU Library. Turn right at the top of the main second-floor stairwell, walk straight ahead, and you will run into the Brain Booth. The relaxing feeling in the Brain Booth envelops the visitor, washing off the mental fatigue of the day." This is how HSU students described the Brain Booth in an article about the recent developments of the initiative in the student newspaper, the *Lumberjack*, from February 27, 2018.

The Brain Booth initiative was received very well by the HSU community as well as the local media. (See the "Library Brain Booth in the News" tab in the *Brain Booth LibGuide* at http://lib guides.humboldt.edu/brainbooth/.) In fall 2016, we conducted a study to explore a broader spectrum of mindfulness activities, which offer intentional brain breaks to students, faculty, and staff. The results reported high levels of interest in this innovative approach among students, and further analysis of patterns of use suggested preferences for certain mindfulness activities. This research study provided evidence to support educators' use of contemplative pedagogy and its value in the information literacy workplace. I presented the study at the 2017 European Conference on Information Literacy in St. Malo, France. The paper, "Dare to Share the Silence: Tools & Practices of Contemplative Pedagogy in a Library Brain Booth," was published in *Information Literacy in the Workplace*, edited by S. Kurbanoglu et al., volume 677 in Springer's Communications in Computer and Information Science series.

Meanwhile, in August 2017, my colleague and Brain Booth partner left HSU. At the beginning of the fall semester, I tried to figure out how to sustain the Brain Booth by myself on top of my other responsibilities as college librarian for the College of Natural Resources and Sciences. I settled on the idea to secure a designated open space for the Brain Booth somewhere in the library and to start circulating Brain Booth equipment for students to check out and use in this space. Luckily, the library dean agreed to give the BB open space on the second floor of the library, and I was able to pilot that idea. During that semester, the Brain Booth circulated two portable biofeedback machines, one light therapy and one sound machine, and two virtual reality goggles (one for each type of cell phone system, iPhone and Android).

The number of checkouts slowly but steadily picked up along the way. I had Brain Booth promotional materials placed throughout the library, including signs listing the Brain Booth equipment available for checkout at the circulation desk.

I also started promoting the Brain Booth at departmental faculty meetings and other forums and began to embed the Brain Booth across the course curricula of different departments. For the first time, students in child development and kinesiology courses visited the Brain Booth during class time in

A Mindful Table

relation to specific course assignments. They engaged with the different stations and had to write a reflection on the activities in relation to their studies and their well-being. Overall, the students acknowledged the positive impact of the approach. They expressed high interest in the new Game-Relax station, which was among the top three preferred activities along with Color-Relax and Biofeedback. The game station offers traditional games as well as, starting last year, a Nintendo Wii with Wii Sports acquired from donations by faculty and staff.

In fall 2017, I also managed to secure a new grant. This allowed me to restore the Brain Booth drop-in hours during the semester by hiring two student assistants to help staff it. After appropriate training, the student assistants were responsible for setting up all the stations in one of the library rooms twice a week and assisting visitors during the drop-in hours. We even added one new activity, an Origami station.

As of now, the Brain Booth hosts weekly drop-in hours as well as provides equipment to check out at the library circulation desk and use at the Brain Booth Designated Open Space (BBDOS). The BBDOS also contains a book and media collection on mindfulness and contemplative pedagogy, as well as coloring supplies, a stationary biofeedback machine, two pedal desks, and a meditation corner with a meditation chair

The BBDOS is next to the room used for setting up all the Brain Booth stations for the drop-in hours and for course assignment time with embedded Brain Booth activities. The course assignments still often include written student reflections on the activities in relation to their studies and their well-being. Students share these reflections with me as part of an ongoing Brain Booth assessment. Most of them point out that the Brain Booth activities are helping them with their focus and overall well-being during rigorous school work as well as in their day-to-day lives.

The Brain Booth student assistants also shared their experiences with the Brain Booth last semester, outlining that one of the most popular activities at the Brain Booth has been the gratitude log, where visitors have the opportunity for self-reflection through words and illustration. The assistants also note that for most visitors, biofeedback machines are new to them, and they are very interested in learning more about them.

Mindfulness in Groups

When asking visitors if they have tried any of the activities we have provided before, most of them respond that they have not but they would like to continue to in the future because it was very enjoyable and beneficial to them.

The interest in the initiative continues to grow in the campus community, and the students and faculty acknowledge the high value of the approach. Last year, the Brain Booth was embedded in the course curricula across the departments of child development and kinesiology, and recreation administration. The school of business joined them the semester after. The departments to follow the next semester were world languages and cultures, and psychology. The Brain Booth initiative shows that librarians are well positioned to adopt mindfulness and contemplative pedagogy and to serve as resources for departmental faculty who may be willing to explore its use in their courses.

I presented on the recent developments of the Brain Booth Initiative at several conferences in 2018, including the International

Mindfulness Together

Conference on Higher Education Advances held in Valencia, Spain, in June and the annual conference of the Society for College and University Planning in Nashville, Tennessee, in July. The best part about the Brain Booth Initiative, though, is as described by Brain Booth student assistant Justina Madrigal:

> The most rewarding part about the Brain Booth has been seeing the transformation of students, from when they first walk in to when they leave. The majority of students come in looking stressed out and gloomy. After trying out the activities that the Brain Booth has to offer, they walk out with smiles on their faces and look renewed and energized. It feels good to be able to contribute to the well-being of the community.

7

Craving Quiet

A Library's Zen Zone

Kellie Sparks and Hillary Fox

F all and spring semesters are especially active at the University of West Florida's John C. Pace Library. As librarians, we observe the usual bustle of students as they find their way through the library halls, clutching a smartphone in one hand and an oversized textbook in the other. However, as each semester progresses, we also begin to feel something in the air. Students are on edge. Their usual smiles are replaced with grimaces. Their leisurely pace is quickened into the awkward gait of a nervous scholar. They are also constantly "plugged-in," whether listening to music from their brightly colored earbuds or playing the latest games from their laptops. This subtle shift signaled to us what we intuitively knew: stress and constant digital engagement would ultimately affect students academically.

Our natural response was to begin researching. We learned that chronic stress can deeply impact the focus, memory, concentration, and creativity of college students. Living without simple quiet moments could be especially detrimental to a student's well-being and mental health. Our concern for the students compelled us to explore remedies that would allow students to experience a brief state of zen.

We began by piloting a library Zen Zone project that introduced the use of the Muse meditation headband. The Muse meditation headband is a device that syncs with a soundscape app. While users listen to the soothing noises of a particular location, the headband captures how active the brain is. During the project, we conducted a pre- and postmeditation survey and collected real-time biofeedback from participants.

The success of this initial project inspired the purchase of additional tools that would enable a multisensory mindful experience. Through research grants, we were able to procure virtual reality headsets, aromatherapy products, mandala coloring books, and other relaxation tools. Similar to how students have different learning styles, we learned that students have different meditation preferences.

The goal of the Zen Zone was threefold: (1) provide tools that could delve into how students physiologically respond to meditation, (2) enable students to improve their perceived level of stress, and (3) allow students to reflect on their meditative experience to assess how their practice could improve.

Preheat

To determine if mindfulness tools in your library are appropriate, the library should gauge the level of interest. This can be achieved by piloting a meditation tool, such as the Samsung Gear VR (virtual reality goggles that incorporate meditation apps) or the Muse meditation headband. A survey that addresses the student's experience, willingness, interest, and preferred meditation device should serve as an assessment tool.

Once the mindfulness oven has fully heated and you have received positive feedback on the pilot project, you can begin investigating which meditation tools are the best fit for your library. During our literature review, we found the following were the most popular ingredients of our mindfulness recipe:

- ▪ VR goggles and a Samsung phone with the "Relax VR" mindfulness app

  In a 2017 study titled "Meditation Experts Try Virtual Reality Mindfulness: A Pilot Study Evaluation of the Feasibility and Acceptability of Virtual Reality to Facilitate Mindfulness Practice in People Attending a Mindfulness Conference" in *Plos One*, Maria Navarro-Haro and colleagues share their belief that using virtual reality can improve your state of mindfulness and assist those who have difficulty focusing their attention.

- Muse meditation headband
- essential oils accompanied by absorbent sticks

  In a 2009 study titled "The Effects of Lavender and Rosemary Essential Oils on Test-Taking Anxiety among Graduate Nursing Students" in *Holistic Nursing Practice*, Ruth McCaffrey, Debra Thomas, and Ann Kinzelmann share that aromatherapy has been shown to lower anxiety levels of graduate students before academic examinations.

- noise-canceling headphones

  In a 2014 article titled "Beliefs about Meditating among University Students, Faculty, and Staff: A Theory-Based Salient Belief Elicitation" in *Journal of American College Health*, Alyssa Lederer and Susan Middlestadt suggest that one of the challenges to practicing meditation and mindfulness is finding a quiet space to do so; noise-canceling headphones provide a solution.

- iPad minis for sound therapy (in the form of apps, spa music, meditation music via YouTube, etc.)

  In a 2017 article titled "Long-Term Music-Listenings' Effects on Blood Pressure, Heart Rate, Anxiety, and Depression" in *Journal of Alternative Medicine Research*, Taunja Bell and David Akombo suggest that music can reduce anxiety and promote health and well-being among individuals.

- mandala coloring pages with colored pencils

  In a 2018 article titled "When Did Coloring Books Become Mindful? Exploring the Effectiveness of a Novel Method of Mindfulness-Guided Instructions for Coloring Books to Increase Mindfulness and Decrease Anxiety" in *Frontiers in Psychology*, Michail Manzios and Kyriaki Giannou share mixed findings on whether mandala coloring pages affect the practice of being mindful, yet they do confirm the reduction of anxiety and improved mood.

Mix all ingredients together to create a Zen Zone.

Bake

Baking times for the Zen Zone will vary by library. To determine the best baking time, or how you will utilize your Zen Zone and evaluate its effectiveness, patron feedback is essential. We gathered patron feedback by setting up a table within the library one day each week during the fall and spring semesters. When students visited, they were asked to complete an electronic survey before and after that captured how the students engaged with the meditation tools and how interested they were in continuing meditation practices. Two versions of a survey were developed: one to capture the experiences of new users and one to capture the experiences of returning users.

NEW USER SURVEYS
Students Who Have Never Used the Zen Zone

PRE-TEST	POST-TEST
How would you rate your current level of stress?	Which tool did you use today?
How familiar are you with the concept of mindfulness?	How would you rate your current level of stress?
How frequently do you practice mindfulness meditation?	If these resources were available during all library hours, how often would you make use of them?
How interested are you in learning more about mindfulness?	How long did you utilize the Zen Zone today?
If the library offered a designed space that provided tools to help you reduce stress and test related anxiety, how interested would you be in using it?	
Where should the designated space be located within the library?	

RETURNING USER SURVEYS
Students Who Are Returning to the Zen Zone

PRE-TEST	POST-TEST
Are you a returning user?	Which tool did you use today?
How would you rate your current level of stress?	How long did you utilize the Zen Zone today?
What tools did you previously use in the Zen Zone this semester?	

The purpose of the surveys was to help determine the participants' preferred mindfulness tools and interest in having a dedicated library space to practice. Participant demographic data including UWF affiliation, year of study, major, and gender were recorded.

FINAL STEP
Taste Your Creation

The final step of designing the Zen Zone is "tasting" the final product. This means reviewing and analyzing the survey data and user interactions to determine how you will move forward. From our "taste test," we learned that participating in the Zen Zone correlated with lower levels of stress immediately after use. The majority of participants rated their stress as a five out of seven in the pre-test, but in the post-test, the majority of participants self-reported a decrease on the stress scale.

Survey results indicated that the most popular items were the high-tech tools: the VR goggles, closely followed by the Muse meditation headband. One noted feature of the VR is the ability for the student to record their heart rate before and after use. While the serene landscapes within the VR app were intended to help students relax, most students reported their heart rate was higher after using the goggles. Many of the participants had never experienced virtual reality and were excited about the novelty of the technology, causing an elevated heart rate. Despite the biofeedback, students using VR still perceived themselves as less stressed after their session.

When asked about the practice of mindfulness, most participants said they were somewhat familiar with the concept, and 63 percent of participants indicated they were "very interested" in learning more about it. When asked about the location of the Zen Zone, the preference among participants was to have a slightly public, designated Zen Zone or to have the Zen Zone located in a private study carrel.

LESSONS LEARNED
Timing Is Everything

Piloting a Zen Zone project for your library requires a knowledge of social patterns within your facility and institution. Knowing the higher traffic times as well as other events at your institution that might affect patrons will have an impact on engaging participants. We perceived Wednesday afternoons as one of the busier times in our library. Each Wednesday during the fall and spring semesters, we set up a Zen Zone table near the entrance of the library where we would assist interested students with using the tools and gather their feedback. The higher patron traffic during this time enabled us to recruit more participants to sample the different meditation tools. We found that between the timing of class changes and with the time it takes to set students up with the technology-based tools, allotting 1.5 to 2 hours for each session allowed ample time for students to visit the station. The highest use times were, ironically, the times of least stress. For instance, during finals, students said they had to study rather than use the Zen Zone.

COOKWARE
Tools You Will Actually Use When Baking

As users explore the various meditation tools, pay attention to what is being requested most frequently. In our case, the novelty of the VR caught the students' interest and ended up being our most-used tool. We encourage those interested in launching their own Zen Zone to consider saving portions of their funding to purchase more of the most popular tools.

Due to the popularity of VR, we used our leftover grant funding to purchase additional goggles and phones.

Further Investigation

An ongoing discussion with the Zen Zone is where to place it permanently within the library and how to sustain the service. Having a designated space would allow more people to practice meditation. However, if the space is not being used, other patrons may take over the space and use it for different purposes. A study carrel repurposed as a meditation room would prevent the space from being misused because students would need to check out a key. The drawback of the small size of the study carrels is that only one or two students could use the space at a time. The discussion of where to place the permanent Zen Zone is one that will continue throughout the pilot project.

Circulation and maintenance policies for the Zen Zone tools are in the developmental stage. Questions surrounding these policies include determining who will house the equipment, whether the circulation desk will become responsible for the Zen Zone technology, how students will figure out how to use the equipment, and what the loan period for each item will be. Answering these questions will involve collaboration between the circulation department and the reference librarians who initiated the Zen Zone. Additionally, as the virtual reality devices and accompanying phones become dated, will additional funding be available to update the technology?

THE ZEN ZONE
Moving Forward

The Zen Zone pilot has shown us that our students' minds crave quiet. Not only have students formally expressed an interest in mindfulness-based stress reduction, but they have verbally praised their meditation experiences after using the Zen Zone. We anticipate that incorporating this type of wellness initiative into the library will positively impact our students once we are able to find an appropriate space and develop policies for its function and sustainability. Once the pilot phase has ended, we plan to continue the research with trial periods that will help us navigate the space and circulation components. In the meantime, this research project has proven to be an incredibly enjoyable experience as we take an active part in providing a way for students to become more mindful within the comfort of a campus environment.

PART
III

Personal Practice

8

Mindful and Reflective Writing as Strategy

How a Work Journal Can Help
Make You Whole

Michelle Reale

*The narrative impulse is always with us;
we couldn't imagine ourselves through
a day without it.*

—Robert Coover

While mindfulness in all aspects of life seems to be all the rage and much lip service is given extolling its usefulness, in my experience, it still seems difficult and problematic for many to implement a sustainable practice—in fact, it seems daunting to many to even try! What many librarians need and can benefit from, both in the long and short term, is a simple strategy that can be performed anywhere and at any time. I am a firm believer in the power of stories—the ability to express our thoughts and feelings in narrative, a form of storytelling where we can be "in the moment" while writing (mindful) and then be able to step back and evaluate what (not how!) we have written about ourselves. *Pen. Paper. Movement across the page. A focusing inward.* As busy professionals, we deserve at least that much for ourselves. Yet so many remain resistant: *I'm not a writer. That isn't the way I think. I've never kept a journal. Where would I find the time?* I have been an advocate for mindfulness journals to colleagues and believe there is value in gentle instruction, in showing what is possible and how one might find the time.

When I was a new librarian, I despaired of two things, in particular: looking foolish in front of a class and being stumped by a question I could not quickly find the answer to. Though my colleagues at the time reassured me, no doubt with good intentions, that neither would happen, in fact, both did—many times over. My own self-doubt often paralyzed me, of course exacerbating each new interaction that my chosen career required. While I feel that I am a naturally reflective person and have kept a journal (I called it a *diary* way back when!) since I was very young, I knew that I needed to develop a strategy that was separate from the daily and copious musings in my notebook. I needed (and this is a word I often use when speaking of journaling and mindfulness) *intentionality* of practice. I needed to create a space for what I was feeling and experiencing at work, in my profession and in relation to my role as an instructor. I needed a deeper awareness that would hopefully grow into a deeper insight. This intentionality was framed by a keen desire to focus inward; to describe, as much as possible, what it was that I was experiencing, how I was feeling about what I was experiencing; and to frame it in narrative form for flow.

This desire was so strong, I remember standing in the Fabriano shop in the airport in Rome and carefully choosing, from among some very delicious and enticing choices, just the right journal—because I was *intentional* about wanting to spend a considerable amount of time with it. I was on my way home and a day away from the workweek, anxiety churning within me, and I vowed to myself to start the journal immediately. I chose a beautiful, large deep-blue journal with slightly textured cream-colored paper. The careful choice of this journal would please and comfort me many times as I would pull it from my book-beaten leather book bag and, on the page, attempt to both understand and silence the inner critic. I let the pen move along the page. That act alone, the motion of the pen across paper in and of itself, is like a meditation. I focused on my breath, the words on the page. I gave myself permission to tell a *story*.

Making It Work

As busy and often already overburdened professionals, not only do we bemoan a lack of time in the course of our days, but we truly lack time—often it seems as if every moment is taken. Then if we should find ourselves with a breather or two in the course of the day, we may not have the mental space and/or energy to be able to make the effort toward an act of mindfulness. The irony here is probably not lost on anyone: when we feel that way, when we have gotten to that point, that is precisely when we actually may need mindfulness the most!

Disabuse yourself of the idea that you need an ocean of time. You don't. Even a few minutes will suffice. You do not need total silence, although it wouldn't hurt; in fact, you don't need conditions to be perfect at all. Start where you are with a notebook and pen. I usually start with a breath and focus on calming my body. Often, the mind will follow. Because I always have so many concerns in the course of my workday—usually focused on some aspect of my classes such as how I am presenting material, my students, and so on—something will quickly arise that I would like to address. When it does, I formulate it into a question, which helps prime a state of mindfulness by giving me something to write *to*. You are now *aware* of something and are becoming focused. When we formulate our thoughts and concerns into questions, we become intentional in practice—we are asking something of ourselves. We write to and for ourselves. We have the opportunity to not only create a story but also later develop a counterstory to our own narrative—which is evidence of growth and problem solving.

What It Looks Like on the Page

As an academic librarian, I have always found information literacy instruction intimidating. I am constantly being called upon to start from scratch with each class that I encounter. I often do not get to see growth in students and am often unaware of how I may (or may not) have helped them. Educator Parker Palmer spoke to the condition as "losing heart" in our teaching and attributes it to the fact that teaching is a "daily exercise in vulnerability." Mindfulness and story help us see that.

August 30, 2016

I was a nervous wreck right before my session. My nerves were amplified because I was being observed. I actually ended up being much calmer than I thought I would be and, because of that, felt that my presentation was much smoother. I felt that I could speak easily and did not experience those awful and humiliating moments of being tongue-tied—or worse, stuttering since my brain always seems to work faster than my mouth. This was a one-shot class—not my favorite for reasons I don't want to go into right now, and I feel that I left so many things unsaid. This causes me such frustration. The website wasn't cooperating and far from the students being disinterested, they seemed to hang on every word. So I let the website go for a bit and engaged them in conversation about how they usually approach research, letting them know it was a "no judgment zone"! This felt good, as they were very forthcoming, which is not always the case. I have to figure out a way to stay focused and fully and completely present in the classroom—and out of it too. Mental fatigue impacts me in so many ways as I am constantly trying to figure out how to engage students. Their inattentiveness is often hard to deal with—sometimes it feels as though I am talking to an empty room. The empty looks are hard to face. But I am still very excited about ideas that I want to implement. I wonder, though, if I will ever stop second-guessing myself about what I know or what I should know. I just want to eventually relax into not being perfect but being the best I can be. The semester is a long one. I need to work on figuring this out.

That entry was written on the first day of the semester. I was assigned a session to teach to a large group of first-year students that were leaving the following week for a semester in London. The first years chosen for this program were highly motivated achievers. I felt my usual anxiety going into the class. After the class, I berated myself as usual, second-guessing everything about the session. I desperately needed the time to be mindful, write, and reflect. My question to myself was "Why do I never feel that I am up to the task?" While this is a broad statement, I felt that it was a necessary place to begin. I would eventually delve into particulars, but I needed to address things in a macro sense. In essence, the passage above contains a bit of everything: a *story* (narrative) about me, my fears and frustrations, and a small victory in the classroom. I am both mindful (focused on my narrative) and reflective, since I wrote this, of course, after the fact.

The Effects of the Journal and Mindfulness

Integrating a journal into your work life can be effective in developing an awareness of your feelings and, subsequently, your actions. It is process rather than product oriented, which may account for some of the resistance I have encountered when talking about it with others. Our perception of time in this fast-paced world where everyone is multitasking is skewed in the wrong direction. We seem not to value something if it does not have a "deliverable" or if it can't be benchmarked, counted, or evaluated. But in fact, I have always believed, and I believe still, that the best resources a library has are the people who work in them. Mindful awareness and reflective journaling can help us to tap into the better part of ourselves with eyes wide open. It is the opposite of acting in the same uninspired and unexamined way that has become the default for so many of us over time.

In this way, I believe that mindfulness and reflective journaling become radical acts, since they disrupt the norm, the default, and gently, though with great intention, move us into a mind-set of greater awareness, not only of ourselves but of those with whom we work (our colleagues) and serve (our students). We decenter ourselves in order to recenter ourselves again. When we can sit with ourselves in the moment, concentrating on our breath while moving the pen across the page, we are on the road to greater clarity of self. We can set assumptions aside and see things—indeed, see ourselves for who and what we really are and what we are capable of—which is, by the way, quite a lot.

John Dewey postulated that learning does not come from experience but instead from the act of *reflecting* on that experience. We integrate the many competing selves in motion when we can settle mind and body. Unplug the technology and grab a pen and a notebook. Take it wherever you think your mind can relax. I have a favorite bench on campus that is set apart from the busiest buildings. It is not a sturdy bench and it continuously flakes paint, but it is situated among many kinds of trees in various stages of growth, along with swaying milkweed plants and sea grass. If I look up, I can see pinpricks of sunlight through the lacy canopy of trees. If it is warm, I might take off my shoes and feel the coolness of the grass beneath my feet. I take a breath and press my feet into earth to ground myself. After I do all of that, sometimes this happens:

November 9, 2016

Today I walked into the quietest class that I have ever encountered. Others' silence has always made me anxious, as if I am not anxious enough already. It is the day after the election and emotions are running high. Did I imagine the pain on the students' faces, or was that my own projection? Instead of panicking, I fiddled around with the computer to give myself time to breathe and steady myself. The professor took his seat, waiting for my presentation. Softly, he said, "Tough day today for everyone, huh?" I nodded. In that moment, I knew I needed to hold a place for what was going on in the class. It would be difficult for them to participate. But I was mindful of what needed to be done and what I could and could not expect from them. They were still quiet, though their faces were receptive. And I am so grateful for that.

9

Mindfulness Is Not a Life Hack

Elizabeth Galoozis and Caro Pinto

Coming to Mindfulness Personally and Professionally

Elizabeth Galoozis: I first came to mindfulness through meditation (via yoga and therapy) . . . it bled into my work last. The idea in meditation about noticing thoughts as they pass rather than judging them is hard for me to do. It's a component of cognitive behavioral therapy to be conscious of thoughts you are having—not just take them at face value but investigate them. I started noticing those thoughts at work—"This is going to go terribly," or "I don't know what I'm talking about," or "These people hate me." Saying them aloud to yourself allows you to examine and investigate those assumptions.

Caro Pinto: Mindfulness started as a personal tool and came into my work later. It's a way to cultivate compassion, especially in one-on-one interactions. I was stressed; I had too much to do. I felt like I had to constantly be *multitasking*. One-on-one interactions felt like interruptions from "work," and I wanted to get them done quickly, asking myself, "How do I get this interaction over with and get back on track?" Engaging with the beginner's mind helped me cultivate compassion, and I remembered that one-on-one interactions *are* the work. I think mindfulness has a rap for being "a relaxation technique," but awareness allows me

This is an edited and condensed conversation between Elizabeth Galoozis and Caro Pinto about mindfulness and its impact on their lives.

to be present in uncomfortable situations, which is not relaxing! Awareness allows me to consider different dimensions within an interaction and ask "Was my affect making it worse?" It allows me to let things slow down and consider the larger experience.

It's Not a Mind Hack for Reference and Instruction

EG: I'm trying to think less about "How am I going to look?" and "Am I going to be able to say that I covered X, Y, and Z?" and tune in more to the classroom. Sometimes I still will ignore awkwardness or tension and forge ahead; it's still a challenge. The idea of the beginner's mind is very resonant to me; I constantly have to remind myself of it during instruction.

Slowing Down and Critically Thinking in Spite of Capitalism

CP: Capitalism programs make us think we have to get through things *fast*. Channeling our feminist comrades, I believe the process is as important as the outcome. Capitalism encourages us to focus on not how we're getting from A to B, just that we've arrived at point B. One might believe, "I have to move as fast as possible. I have to be efficient." When you don't have compassion for where people are, when they might not be ready to hear what you're saying, it's easy to leave people behind. I try to focus less on forging ahead and more on creating space for students to ask questions.

EG: You and I both work with high-achieving students who may still be in the competitive mind-set that got them admitted. I'm in awe of what the students I work with have accomplished. I hope that a mindful approach says to them, "At least for the time you spend with me, you can admit the things that you don't know." Hopefully, we are holding that space. In my own college education, I feel the most important things I learned were how to think critically and how to reflect. That's why I appreciate questions that I might have thought of in the past as challenging or problematic, like when students ask "why" about processes or structures. In the past, I would want to move on quickly and get to searching or keywords. Now I hope that students ask those reflective questions.

CP: We're focused on the outcome: "Did this work?" We don't know if things worked right away. My work with eportfolios has taught me that we tend to learn whether it "worked" years later. Students might say, "It was annoying when we had to make those portfolios. In retrospect, it was great because I had the space to think." Now I realize when they are in the "annoying" moment, they are stressed.

EG: Do you think that using words like "meditation" and "mindfulness" set off that "life hack" switch?

CP: Perhaps. I think bringing mindfulness into my teaching is a part of the arc of my career. I think by not using a signifier like "Buddhism" or "mindfulness," I am trying to acknowledge that teaching and learning are hard without evangelizing about mindfulness. I've been teaching in some way for almost fifteen years and I've cultivated a set of practices over that time. In 2005, I learned to read students when I was a teaching assistant leading weekly discussions. I had a section that would not talk. This was premindfulness. Eventually, I said, "Listen, I'm going to sit here and stare at you until you talk." I stared at them for nearly fifty minutes. They talked the next time. That's pretty combative, but staring back at them for fifty minutes taught me that I could gauge their levels of discomfort through observation. I've taught myself to tune into uncomfortable moments and adjust. Learning to teach is a lifelong process. Mindfulness informs how I respond, whether things are going well or poorly.

EG: I think it's analogous to other instructional things—like active learning—having a mind-set is the most important thing. You can't just pull it out unless you already have the mind-set of "I'm going to pay attention to what's going on."

CP: Mindfulness is not a trick. It's not a one-off thing. It's part of the process of creating conditions for learning.

Vulnerability

CP: Vulnerability is hard. I think that many of my students organize their time in ways that make reflection difficult.

Their lives can feel destination oriented. In my experience, we don't create enough space for students to think about "why." That "why" can help provide a framework for an engaged life.

EG: How do you actually go about doing that in an instructional situation?

CP: I use breathing exercises and visualizations. There's usually some eye rolling, but I always notice palpable relief in their bodies. We can acknowledge that being in a classroom can be messy and stressful. It's an invitation to say, "You're bringing a lot to this moment; so, let's take ten breaths." It reminds me of a rowing crew. During sprints, our coxswain would help us visualize what would happen. The visualizations reminded us why we were rowing and who we were rowing for. In class, I'll say "We're going to take ten breaths. We're going to take one breath for your classmate to the left of you, for the classmate to the right of you," and I continue in this vein until we've reached ten people/places/ideas to breathe for collectively. Breathing can be a reset.

Discomfort

EG: I want to talk about a time I think I failed at being mindful. I taught two sessions the day after the 2016 presidential election. I told the instructor, "I'm happy to abandon my lesson plan, and we can just talk." She said she thought I should go ahead as planned. You didn't have to be mindful to notice that people were upset. Eventually, when we started talking about their topics, because all of their topics were about social justice, I could tell that their energy was changing. I ignored it at the beginning, partially because I know we have conservative students on campus and I didn't want to get into it with them. But I feel like I should have at least at the beginning acknowledged *something*. Something like, "This is a strange day for a lot of us, so I know it might be hard to concentrate, but let's try to direct our thoughts to something else." I struggle with acknowledging discomfort in a classroom. I'm too literal about it, thinking I'd have to say "I'm going to name discomfort now." So I'm curious to hear about how you go about that in a subtler way.

CP: I'll go around and ask, "Does anyone have any questions?" There's the power dynamic, and I don't want to make any assumptions about what's happening. It's about reading people: What are their faces doing? Are they making eye contact? I think sometimes students feel like they should already be fully formed people. They've had to do so much to get into an elite college, and when they arrive, they suddenly have to contend with other aspects of being a person.

On Using Mindfulness at Work

There's the interpersonal, and then there's
just like your way of being at work.
—Caro Pinto

Meetings

EG: Let's talk about meetings.
CP: Meetings are *hard*. People can act out in all kinds of ways.
EG: There's so much uncertainty.
EG: It's hard to stay mindful or cultivate compassion when no one else is with you. You can bring students with you, but it's harder with colleagues. I have occasionally suggested taking a break in a meeting . . . not breathing but refocusing. There's also the tension that there are deadlines and decisions have to be made. A meeting that's all about process could be seen as a failure.

Holding Space to Create Boundaries

CP: I think it's hard when we don't set boundaries with people. I had a difficult conversation recently with someone, and in spite of the discomfort, I didn't dissociate; I breathed and said what I thought. Mindfulness is not a shortcut. In some cases, you invite conflict or a longer conversation. It's not a timesaver, but you might have a better outcome from engaging in a longer process that explores more of the issues.
EG: There's always a tension between thinking "I can move through this thing" and feeling like you're starting to take abuse or be worn down.
CP: Everyone needs to have their own way of redirecting conversations.

Back to Capitalism

CP: Returning to the rhetoric around mindfulness and productivity, I used to dissociate from everything and complete many tasks. Mindfulness made me more thoughtful. When I didn't have secure employment, I felt like I had to do *everything*. Now that I have stable employment, I don't do as much social media because I don't feel like I need to perform my value in the same way. That's a privilege. Does precarity make us disassociated? Mindfulness can make us more embodied, help us consider what we are doing and why.

EG: You know, it's possible to follow that thread and say something like, "Mindfulness is a luxury," or, "It's not for the precarious."

CP: Mindfulness can be a tool in precarity; it was for me. I didn't immediately notice how stable employment buoyed my mental health. I was relieved, but I did not notice the cumulative effect until a year later. I began to say no to some things to create space for others. I redirected my energies.

EG: Productivity is different for different people in different contexts.

CONCLUSION
On Not Performing Mindfulness

CP: Why do we feel like we have to *perform* mindfulness? I like the mantra "Simply begin again." *Tricycle Review* has a daily digest. On April 16, 2018, it featured this quote from Shunryu Suzuki Roshi, "When you forget all your dualistic ideas, everybody becomes your teacher, and everything can be the object of worship." When you're curious, anything has the potential to become your teacher.

EG: Tell me more about the curiosity approach.

CP: It makes things take another beat. It's an opportunity for people to apologize or redirect their comments or just check in.

EG: It can be really hard, whether in the classroom or workplace, to not simply react. To take a second and seek to understand rather than seek to be understood.

CP: It gives people an opportunity to see what they mean and experience empathy on both sides and not get attached to being right.

10

Outreach for Inreach

Using Digital Resources
to Promote Mindfulness

Jenn Carson

When we think of doing outreach programs in libraries, we generally picture an enthusiastic librarian or paraprofessional going out into the community armed with books, pamphlets, program calendars, and perhaps even a tablet or laptop to do online registrations. Outreach is an opportunity to show off our programming and presentation skills outside the four walls of the library and entice potential clients to want to spend more time accessing our services. One program that is becoming more and more popular and requested in libraries (public, academic, and otherwise) is meditation and/or mindfulness training. It's no wonder that according to a 2015 National Center for Health Statistics report on comprehensive health services, 8.0 percent of US adults practice mindfulness and meditation. Compare that with only 6.9 percent of people accessing massage therapy or 9.5 percent practicing yoga and you can get a feel for how widespread its use is. The interesting thing is, we see advertisements for yoga studios and subsequent lifestyle purchases (mats, blocks, clothing, videos, etc.) everywhere, but the practice of meditation, while almost equally popular, seems to be (fittingly, perhaps?) quieter.

There are probably several reasons for this. For one, mindfulness is, in general, a less marketable activity. You don't need any props, classes, fancy pants, or exotic retreats (though these are all nice!) to participate. It's just you, and your breath, and your thoughts. It can be done anywhere, anytime, by anyone.

Once people receive basic instruction, they are good to go, and this is where the library comes in by providing books, CDs, programs, and outreach opportunities. And for those patrons that prefer ongoing support for their mindfulness practices, the library can be an excellent resource by offering recurring programs, like a weekly meditation meet-up (online or in person) or monthly mindfulness book clubs or by referring patrons to services in the community, such as silent retreats, lectures on the subject, Zen or Shambhala centers, or secular *sanghas* (communities of practitioners). One of the other reasons mindfulness may be less visible than its more show-offy cousin, westernized yoga (in sharp contrast to traditional eight-limbed yoga practice, the goal of which is enlightenment, not looking hot in stretchy pants), is that the practice is, by nature, more inwardly focused and accessible to people of all body types, physical abilities, and levels of health.

There are many program delivery options for offering meditation and mindfulness programs on-site, some of which are discussed in this book; others are available in my own forthcoming book through Rowman & Littlefield, *Yoga and Meditation at the Library: A Practical Guide for Librarians* (slated for release in 2019). What I want to discuss here is how we reach our audience, or potential audience, in more out-of-the-box, technology-driven ways. People are living increasingly plugged-in and digital lives, which many studies have shown has left us with shorter attention spans and difficulties with delayed gratification, both impediments (though not impossibilities!) for the mindfulness practitioner and also the teacher. Scientists call our constant multitasking "continuous partial attention." I'm sure you are familiar with the phenomenon: ever check your phone while on your computer while also listening to music and/or eating a snack? Me too. That's OK; we've got to start somewhere. As we remind ourselves in our fleeting moments of clarity, we must work with what we have—and who we are—and when life is approached with this attitude, everything and everyone can be our guide. There is great comfort in supporting—and being supported by—others embarking on this inward journey. These brave souls are referred to as bodhisattvas (mindful warriors) in the Buddhist tradition, but famous ABC anchorman, meditator, and best-selling author Dan Harris mockingly labels us (himself included) as "fidgety skeptics." Despite having disciplined solo practices, this sense of belonging is also one of the reasons meditators traditionally gather together, especially in the Buddhist lineages, and join a *sangha*, whether as a loose-fitting group of like-minded associates that meet on a regularly scheduled basis or in a more structured organization, such as a monastery. For our purposes, as librarians, we want to be careful to build a secular, accessible community of practitioners from various backgrounds and experience levels, and if we want to connect with our patrons (and staff!) and support their mindfulness practices, we also have to go to where they are—online.

The benefits of online mindfulness resources are many, including a seemingly unlimited reach thanks to sharing on social media platforms, around the clock access, and the relatively low-cost to use and, in some cases, produce these tools. Some more nuanced benefits to consider may be how the anonymity of an online platform allows people with social phobias to access the services and join in the conversation at their own discretion, how those with limited access to transportation or limited mobility can use digital resources from home, and how those with sensory issues can access the information in a way that may feel more comfortable for them.

What are the drawbacks of online mindfulness resources? For one, not all online mindfulness resources are free—or if they are, it may only be for a trial period. Such is the case for the Headspace app. Others have a sliding fee scale (the Mindfulness app, for example, is $9.99/month to $59.99/12-month membership); this may be cost prohibitive to many patrons. Online mindfulness training courses, such as the eight-week Mindful Mood Balance course, which is $400.00 for the first three months, can also be expensive. The ToDo Institute offers a thirty-day online mindfulness training program for $93.00, which is more reasonable, and a quick Google search will reveal that there are many, many more available through other institutions. The problem is, you don't always get what you pay for. The brain-training game Luminosity was recently fined two million dollars for deceptive advertising. Some online courses—such as the Be Mindful Online Mindfulness Course, which has been vetted by both the University of Oxford and the UK's Mental Health Foundation (and at $95.00, is reasonably priced)—have a proven track record for being effective, but many others do not. Another barrier to use is that not everyone has access to digital devices or Internet access at home. According to a 2016 Pew Research Center study, 73 percent of US residents have broadband Internet access at home, leaving 27 percent of citizens to find other ways to get connected. This is one of the services libraries are providing by having free Wi-Fi, public access computers, and even preloaded iPods with yoga sequences or guided meditation ready for in-house use. But this doesn't alleviate the barriers facing people that don't have the mobility or means to come to the library to use these services. In some cases, libraries that are already offering books-by-mail services are expanding these offers to also mail out audiobooks, DVDs, Playaways, and even Daisy players and discs.

Staying Grounded

As librarians—not doctors or medical researchers—we have to be careful not to oversell the promise of mindfulness and meditation. While we may be practitioners ourselves and may be keen to share the benefits we have reaped in our own lives, we need to be mindful (pun intended) not to assume those benefits will be transferable to others who may be on very different journeys and working from very different places. Zindel Seigal, director of clinical training in the Graduate Department of Clinical Psychological Science at the University of Toronto Scarborough and developer of the above-mentioned Mindful Mood Balance course, is cautious about people with preexisting mental health conditions, such as depression or anxiety, jumping into using mindfulness apps; they often have a very hard time disidentifying with their own thinking and may feel like failures if it doesn't come easily, which may only compound their preexisting symptoms. Dan Harris experiences this firsthand in his book, *10% Happier: How I Tamed the Voice in My Head, Reduced Stress without Losing My Edge, and Found Self-Help That Actually Works—a True Story*. In it, he finds doing loving-kindness meditation (also called compassion practice) nearly impossible while suffering from depression because it is very difficult to show any kindness toward yourself (or sometimes others) when you are feeling so grossly inadequate. It fact, it only made him feel worse, unless he started healing from the depression.

So what is the best way to get these resources into the hands of your patrons? Creating a curated digital resource list of mindfulness materials for your website and/or online catalog is a great start, and make sure to advertise it on your social media channels and perhaps even in your print or other marketing campaigns, if you have them. Consider creating a bookmark to hand out at the circulation or reference desk for enquiring minds or to use during relevant programs. Consider doing a promo video talking up your list of online resources and sharing it on your institution's YouTube channel and Facebook page. While you're at it, why not create a short mindfulness video or podcast your patrons can download and follow along with? It's not difficult, and you probably already have all the equipment you need at work: a camera to record the video or microphone to record the audio and some free, simple audio/video editing software, such as iMovie (for Mac) or OpenShot (for Windows, Mac, and Linux). Create a basic script to follow along. The video or podcast doesn't need to be long—in fact, the shorter and more concise it is, the more likely your patrons will give it a whirl or use it regularly. Try to keep it five to fifteen minutes long. You can see a sample mindfulness video I created for my library colleagues to help them de-stress at their desks here: www.jenncarson.com. You could even try hosting your own online meditation session by using free web conferencing software, such as Zoom or Google Hangouts.

Additional Resources

Here's a sampling of some librarian-approved, tried-and-tested digital resources you can feel confident recommending to your patrons or using yourself—for reference, program development, or just taking a much-needed zen break. They aren't all secular, but you can pick and choose what mindfulness tools you take from them.

Blogs/Websites

Elephant Journal
www.elephantjournal.com

Lion's Roar: Buddhist Wisdom for Our Time
www.lionsroar.com

Mindful: Healthy Mind, Healthy Life
www.mindful.org

The On Being Blog
https://onbeing.org/blog/

Tricycle: The Buddhist Review
https://tricycle.org

Yoga in the Library
www.yogainthelibrary.com

Free Applications (for iOS and Android)

Aura
www.aurahealth.io

Insight Timer
https://insighttimer.com

Stop, Breathe, Think
www.stopbreathethink.com

Podcasts

Hello Humans
http://hellohumans.co

The One You Feed
www.oneyoufeed.net

Waking Up
https://samharris.org/podcast/

Online Videos

"All It Takes Is 10 Mindful Minutes" by Andy Puddicombe
    www.ted.com/talks/andy_puddicombe_all
    _it_takes_is_10_mindful_minutes/

"Meditation 101: A Beginner's Guide" by Happify
    www.youtube.com/watch?v=o-kMJBWk9E0/

"Mindfulness Animated in 3 Minutes"
by AnimateEducate
    www.youtube.com/watch?v=mjtfyuTTQFY/

"Self-Transformation through Mindfulness"
by Dr. David Vago
    www.youtube.com/watch?v=1nP50edmzkM/

"A Simple Way to Break a Bad Habit"
by Judson Brewer
    www.ted.com/talks/judson_brewer_a_simple
    _way_to_break_a_bad_habit/

"Why Mindfulness Is a Superpower:
An Animation" by Happily
    www.youtube.com/watch?v=w6T02g5hnT4/

11

Mindfully Managing Library Teams

Jenny Colvin

Mindfulness can be a tool in any interpersonal interaction. Being able to quickly accept what is happening in the present moment is always a good place to start, particularly in moments of unanticipated stress, change, and conflict. While my personal practice has a powerful effect on many areas of my life, I've also used mindfulness concepts when managing a library team.

Using Strengths to Build a Team

When the Furman University Libraries restructured in 2012, it was the first time we had a division known as Outreach Services. Outreach Services encompasses instruction, reference, all liaison roles, and the librarians in the branch libraries. As the newly appointed assistant director for Outreach Services, it was also my first time in any type of management role. We decided to employ Clifton StrengthsFinder®, facilitated by a trainer on our campus, as a team-building activity. Knowing your strengths can be useful to an individual, but I was more interested in exploring the impact on the team. To begin with, we explored our strengths as individuals by taking a test and reading about the five strengths that resulted. Then, through various exercises, we paired up with people who shared our strengths to discuss how we were similar and then with people in the group with a different strength to talk about what a partnership between those two strengths would look like. One person was identified as the person you should consult with when planning a new initiative because she was likely to be able to identify solutions to potential problems.

Our growing understanding of strengths and their intersections has been an underpinning in our team ever since. I found it useful to have a shared vocabulary to clearly communicate in specific situations, for instance when and why another person might need to be brought into a discussion, in understanding the type of information another person might require before making a decision, or in anticipating how a person with a specific strength might approach a conflict or disagreement. Clifton StrengthsFinder is one tool that can provide this assistance in building a working shared language within a group.

We then looked at the group as a whole (using the Team Strengths Grid) and how our strengths were grouped among the broader categories—Executing, Influencing, Relationship-Building, or Strategic Thinking. We had surprisingly few strengths in the Influencing category, and we discussed how this might have an impact on moments where we needed advocacy and support. This led us to a discussion about ways we could use the strengths we did have to compensate for this lack while also identifying potential partnerships outside our group that might enhance our services. It was also clear to me that the one person who had most of her strengths in Executing might feel burned out since so few of us had strengths in that category. I have been more intentional in checking in with her about this issue specifically and adjusting work expectations accordingly.

These were useful discussions and we enjoyed having them, and when we had one librarian leave and thus the opportunity to hire someone new, discussion of not just the strengths of the candidates but what they would bring to our team became more prevalent. As this goes to publication, we are embarking on a new hiring process and will continue this conversation, even six years later.

Strengths Enhanced through Reflection

One year after first discovering our strengths, I prepared a page of reflection questions for our conversation during brunch at an Outreach Services retreat.

1. What do you remember about your strengths? Jot it down. (Note: I brought the grid with me in case someone forgot!)
2. What do you do within Outreach Services that you feel aligns with your strengths?
3. What do you do within Outreach Services that you feel is at odds with your strengths?
4. In an ideal world, what would you like to see happen with the job responsibility from question 3?

My approach is a hybrid, using strengths-based reflection and employing the job demands-resources model. The job demands-resources model gives employees an opportunity to define as much of their work as possible, to increase buy-in and decrease burnout. I was particularly interested in this last reflection question as a means to both of these objectives, creating a pathway to allow the members of my team to still accomplish the same work and provide the same services as a unit but also shifting tasks internally to address feelings of burnout for individuals.

We had a long discussion about these questions after each person had the opportunity to write out their thoughts. Since many of us have similar work responsibilities, there was already a fair amount of flexibility in the division of labor. Sometimes all of us shared the work in an area (such as research assistance), while other times one person would take on the majority of responsibility for a task or project (such as planning a workshop). Through these conversations, we discovered that some people were doing work that caused them stress or distress, and it was work that others in the group were interested in—they just hadn't volunteered because they perceived the other person as being personally invested in the work.

One librarian with her own college-aged children expressed that she was no longer enjoying working with student groups and, in an ideal world, would stop doing that part of outreach for a time. Another person expressed how one task gave her considerable anxiety and that she would prefer to not have to generate the content for that particular task. In both situations, and other similar situations, the group shifted work. All members of Outreach Services who took on new work during this discussion were doing so not out of obligation or to help out a coworker but because it was work he or she genuinely enjoyed and did not mind taking on. I was careful to make sure that nobody was only taking on more work but that it was more of a trade. For example, one person who wanted to teach less volunteered to become the point person for tutorials. We made changes that seemed small from the outside, since the same work was being accomplished, but it made a significant change in morale.

This entire process—reflection, discussion, shift—happened in one retreat session before lunch. I believe the process worked this quickly because of our foundational work of building the team and establishing trust. We do not always have the luxury of only doing work we love. However, a manager who intentionally builds to strengths and addresses burnout can start by asking team members to reflect on questions like those above. From a mindfulness perspective, first a manager must *notice* that members of this team may be experiencing burnout. From there, a manager can *facilitate* a mode of reflection and discussion that allows all members of the team to see that issue as a group challenge. Last but not least, a manager can *assess* the changes as they evolve, to see whether situations have improved. Not all tasks can be eliminated or shifted, but team members will feel the positive impact of the attention. Attention paired with action is the sweet spot.

Celebrating Failures (and Successes)

Part of attention to task shifting is a willingness to try something new. Sometimes changes just work, and sometimes they require additional effort. The theory behind celebrating failure has to do with cultivating an environment of creativity and risk without punishment or other negative consequences. If we have failed, that means we have dared to try something that was not a guarantee, that was not proven. It is these risks that end in successes and breakthroughs, but it is also a given that not everything can succeed the first time.

In an attempt to celebrate risk-taking and to normalize the failure that accompanies it, I made the leap to a flat-out celebration of failures. Every year, my group gathers for a retreat (it is essential that everyone can be there). I try to hold the celebration in a space with at least a whiteboard; our favorite is a room lined with whiteboard paint. I give everyone some time to think about their own most spectacular failure and most shining success from the previous year. They are encouraged to select something work-related but also can use an example from their personal lives if they want. Of course, deciding what to share is up to each team member. If there is something truly horrible that they are too embarrassed by, they can refrain from sharing it. Most of the time, because of the trust established between team members, they are not reluctant to be vulnerable.

Similar to a popular party game, we all draw our failures and successes on the whiteboards with markers. If there is only one whiteboard, we take turns. The idea is to try to guess the failure they are drawing as the picture is revealed. Depending on the sensitivity of the members in a team, it may not be the best strategy to guess someone's failure. In that case, try guessing what is being drawn and let the artist explain what the drawing is of and what it represents.

I encourage people to start by drawing the failure and end with the success. Revisiting the failure can bring up dormant emotions that are still sensitive. After several years of this prac-tice, I have seen the group response to the failure go one of two ways. Most of the time, the reactions of others serve to diffuse the strength of a failure. "It wasn't so bad" or "I didn't notice this at all" might be common reactions, or sometimes another library faculty or staff member can point out how that event or issue helped connect to a new idea, an improvement, or the building of a relationship. At first, I was nervous about this diffusion of concerns; I worried people would feel like they were not being heard. Instead, I have seen how this practice builds trust between team members. These days, they seem to feel comfortable shar-ing reflections on less-than-perfect outcomes. If mistakes are openly shared, the rest of us can more quickly mobilize to pro-vide support or assistance.

Every once in a while, there will be a failure that cannot be diffused. Maybe it really is as bad as the person felt it was. Maybe there was simply no way to improve the situation. Maybe they couldn't save it. Maybe after it happened, they didn't want to get back on the horse or teach that class or work with that faculty member again. This can feel tricky or like the game is failing. Mindfulness is key in this moment. Mindfulness in the face of failure acknowledges that *this happened*. In a moment where everything is going wrong, mindfulness creates community by saying, "I've had that feeling before, and now I'm here." When sharing a failure, mindfulness allows us to go through it together rather than alone. The only way out is through.

An unanticipated side effect of this is that when a similar situation arises or a person involved in that moment resurfaces, the rest of the group knows the stakes and feelings involved, and all of us can be better colleagues for one another. Awareness breeds attention.

Sharing a failure, while often a moment of unity, can also leave a person feeling vulnerable and exposed. This is when the celebration of successes can step in. Some people are not inclined to point out their own achievements, but an official celebration allows them a brief moment to bask in appreciation from others who understand the amount of work involved and what it might mean for that person and to ensure that achievement is properly acknowledged.

While this exercise can be scaled to a larger group, perhaps an entire library, I think you will find it is most effective in smaller groups with an established relationship built on trust. If people feel underappreciated, misunderstood, or particularly unsuccessful, they may be less inclined to be vulnerable.

Managing with Mindfulness

The power of attention, the power of acceptance—mindfulness provides a person managing a library team with many tools. By modeling these practices and creating space for them, the team will strengthen from the inside out.

PART
IV

Teaching/
Research

12

Shifting the Pace

Contemplative Practices and
the Research Process

Lisa Meléndez

O n a daily basis, librarians observe how rapidly
changing technologies impact the ways students
interact with information and approach doing research. For many, particularly at a community college, busy life-
styles coupled with information overload uproot the time needed
for critical engagement with material. I frequently encounter
beleaguered students struggling to integrate (or "shove" as one
student said the other day) required sources into "finished" papers
or starting to write new ones before reading or digesting materials. Their stress and time constraints led me to turn to my training in yoga studies to see how I might shift their experience of
research into a more meaningful process.

Finding overlap between particular principles of yoga and
information literacy skills, I designed the following assignments
to expose students in LIB 101: Introduction to College Research
(a semester-long course) to a variety of contemplative tools while
learning how to locate, evaluate, and synthesize information.
Beginning with a broad theme such as "stress management" or
"mindfulness," each student was responsible for modifying the
topic according to his or her own interests or major over the
course of the semester. The students also understood that they
themselves would be a primary source of information along the
way. My next step was to create a variety of opportunities so
students could incorporate different tools into other areas of
their academic and personal lives. In essence, I wanted students

to interact with information in ways that validated their own experiences—shifting from familiar yet seemingly stressful patterns to a pace that encouraged engagement with the oftentimes messy, uncertain process of exploration and discovery. While the practices were first developed for LIB 101, I repurposed the exercises as a guest speaker in the course "College Seminar" and in the Human Services program's Seminar and Field Practicum course. The practices also worked well outside the traditional classroom when I offered them during a workshop for the college's annual Creative Writing Festival and the Tri-campus Student Leadership conference.

Journaling

The Tree Observation Journal was one of the first practices I developed after participating in the Association for the Contemplative Mind in Higher Education's summer session. Held annually at Smith College, the session offers participants diverse opportunities to explore and develop ways of bringing contemplative methods into the classroom and onto campus. Giving instructions that were intentionally minimal, I asked the students to choose one tree on campus to sit with and observe over the course of twelve weeks. They were to spend three to five minutes a week with the same tree, then write or draw about the experience in a small notebook I distributed to each student. Both external (tree) and internal (self) observations were encouraged, as was being consistent, open, and nonjudgmental. After reviewing the notebooks, I used additional prompts to facilitate a discussion in which students revisited and reflected on their entries. For example, I asked them to consider how their initial reactions might have changed over time, to which one student remarked, "Taking five minutes out of my day seemed pointless but somewhat educational. I learned a lot about other students gossiping about life issues, and I [take] the time to listen to my own thoughts." Another prompt asked them to reflect on how they chose their tree. Did they take time, perhaps walking around campus to unknown areas, or did they pick the first, most convenient tree? I also asked them to consider the vocabulary they used to describe their experience; did their word choices reflect expectations or emotions? The prompts were offered to bring awareness to how the experience might point to other patterns, or *saṁskāra,* in their lives. Despite some initial uneasiness with brief guidelines as opposed to rigid requirements, their entries began to deepen over time:

> Standing half full, the bark looks like its shredding with stripes peeling the color of a pale yellow. On the roots are fallen branches. Maybe my tree is a late bloomer—is it shredding the worn branches to make the remaining ones stronger to withhold the winter months?

> ■ ■ ■

> Today I am thinking about what I cannot see. I'm looking into the ground, thinking about how the roots must be very strong. How will my tree survive this winter? Does it have everything it needs, or is it like me, who looks different than my neighbor? I have everything I need even though, compared to many women, I may look frail too.

> ■ ■ ■

> Looking at my tree for over an hour. Dozens just walk by and don't pay any attention to my tree.

> ■ ■ ■

> I hate being out in the cold, so sitting by my tree was hard today. At least I can escape the cold. Trees can't, and that's a weird thought.

> ■ ■ ■

> The tree is starting to lose leaves quickly. I could never be a tree—that would be like losing your hair when it got cold. It must stink to lose something that is a part of you for so long. That thought made me sad. I'm done now.

> ■ ■ ■

> My tree had another tree leaning on it, but it seemed to be stronger. Was it my wishful thinking? Although it didn't plan on another tree falling on it, it stays strong because it has to. A few branches will not hurt at all.

■ ■ ■

> I haven't seen my tree in two weeks, and it's sad to see it bare, with no leaves and no friends around. Sometimes I feel my tree shares my feelings. The past few weeks have been rough and now back to reality. Like me, my tree will begin to become more lively as time passes.

In general, students' initial observations tended to focus on the physicality of the tree. However, by intentionally setting aside just a small amount of regular time to quietly sit, observe, and write, their thoughts deepened, suggesting an interruption of expectations, or autopilot, and a shift toward a more mindful presence. Because our relationship with information affects who we are and who we become, the tree journal practice was designed to give students the opportunity to connect with a particular object over time in order to then consider how they take in and digest information. Sitting with the same tree regularly gave them the space and time to essentially meditate on the tree and observe change by practicing discernment, similar to developing skills in concentration and critical evaluation. Further, engaging in an activity that was unfamiliar offered them an opportunity for self-reflection—and possibly a glimpse into their own ways of seeing themselves and the world around them.

Other Approaches

Another practice I developed worked well for a talk I provided for the Seminar and Field Services Practicum course. My topic centered on research methods in the field as well as self-care and stress management. Being adult learners, as opposed to traditional college-age students, many in the program were returning to complete a degree or begin a new career while already holding down jobs and caring for families. As such, I chose a silent, technology-free walk around campus that would be slow paced and last fifteen to twenty minutes. Before exiting the classroom, I asked the class to leave their belongings behind in the locked classroom so that they could walk as freely and as lightly as possible (with the exceptions of phones or other devices in case of medical or family concerns). Before starting, I gave simple guidelines: Follow my lead, practice silence, observe your surroundings using all your senses, and acknowledge others with gesture rather than sound. If I stop to observe, do the same, and along the way, take note of your feelings, state of mind, and bodily reactions. While meandering, because I was open to changing course, I used gestures to prompt awareness, like pointing to my nose while inhaling deeply under the pine trees or to my ears when stepping over dry leaves and pods. I also incorporated moments of stillness, like stopping in front of a building that reflected our images or at the base of a large staircase.

When we returned to the classroom, the quiet, contemplative mood that lingered was conducive to doing reflective writing. The following comments come from this writing:

> I got to walk around campus to places I've never been before—or rather never had to have gone before. It was very different to walk around just for the purpose of observing. It allowed me to notice things I wouldn't have noticed normally.

■ ■ ■

> It was at a great time of rush, rush, rush on a Monday. To just *stop, be quiet, walk, look, and listen* calmed the whole world down—well, my whole world.

■ ■ ■

> I enjoyed being able to appreciate nature and the silence without being in a rush to go somewhere. Walking and freewriting gave me a chance to reflect on my thoughts and feelings.

■ ■ ■

> We just walked with no real purpose besides being relaxed and walking. It gives you time to step back from everything and really calm yourself, making it easier to deal with stress later on.

For those who find it difficult to sit quietly, a simple practice like a silent walk offers a practical, accessible way to refresh or transition between work, home, and school. As discussed, because the walk doesn't have to be long, it can be incorporated into one's routine—for example, walking to and from class. The only requirement is to do so with intention. While no one in this group was physically challenged, the exercise could be modified accordingly.

Other experiential components that were included in this class made up of future social workers were the "Just like Me" compassion meditation and breathing exercises combined with *nyāsam,* or gesture. To practice this technique,

- rest the hands in the lap with the palms facing up;
- place each thumb at the base of the first finger on each hand and slowly slide the thumb up the finger while inhaling;
- after the natural pause, slowly slide the thumb back down the same finger while exhaling; and
- after the next natural pause, move the thumb to the base of the next finger and repeat technique, moving from finger to finger with each round of breath.

Toward the end of the semester, I reached out to the practicum professor to survey the students about which tools resonated with them. A sample of their feedback follows:

Walking silently outdoors was the best one for me because it made me look at nature and birds, and that made me forget about everything else. Afterward, I took my kids walking and we walked without talking, and then we discussed what we saw and liked about the walk.

■ ■ ■

Combining thumbsliding with breathing helped me de-stress in the moment. I used it in my abnormal psych class when I felt overwhelmed about upcoming finals. It really lowers my stress and makes me feel relaxed. I wish I had this when I first made the transition from high school to college.

■ ■ ■

Because I have anxiety, *nyāsam* helped me relax by distracting my mind. The only thought I had was sliding my thumb. I feel a lot of kids would benefit from it because school is stressful.

While the previous practice used silence to encourage students to see with "new eyes," known as *pratipakṣa bhāvanām* in yoga, another practice used sound to focus and calm the mind, creating a space for creativity. Designed for a workshop during the English department's Creative Writing Festival, I used similar exercises for workshops in public libraries, as well as the aforementioned student leadership conference. To begin, I taught participants the *ujjāyī* breathing technique, which produces a subtle sound to make the breath more tangible. Once comfortable with the technique, I asked participants to link each round of breathing with *nyāsam* as described above. The coordination of all parts of the breath, including the natural pauses, requires attention, which calms the mind with repetition; this exercise also helps warm up the fingers for writing. With the eyes closed, after twelve or so breaths, I asked participants to relax their hands into their laps or place them on their lower belly and listen as I read a poem aloud, first in English, then in Spanish. The poem, "Here I Sit . . . By An Open Window / Heme aquí . . . sentando junto a una ventana abierta," written by Jesús Papoleto Meléndez and translated into Spanish by Caroline Fung Feng, appears in Papoleto's collected works, *Hey Yo! Yo Soy! Forty Years of Nuyorican Street Poetry* (2012). Breathing deeply and listening actively, the participants were encouraged to hear the words as sounds, familiar and unfamiliar at the same time. After the reading, I moved into a guided visualization based on the poem's title—that is, sitting by an open window—and then asked them to open their eyes and begin writing.

Putting It All Together

The assignments, or "recipes," described here grew out of the connection I see between contemplative practices and the research process. By exposing students (and others) to tools that encourage a slower, calmer pace for engaging with information, I believe we are preparing them to thrive in our information-saturated, fast-paced world. By beginning with themselves as a source of information, they can validate their own experiences while offering meaningful encounters with observation, sustained focus, discernment, reflection, and other skills. As contemplative practices and research are processes, it is important to begin where one is to move forward intelligently and mindfully; in yoga, this is referred to as *viñyāsa krama*. Positioned on the front lines of information services and technology, librarians can use our talents and passions to build on the lifelong skills we teach. By meaningfully connecting people with information, we fulfill our profession's essential role.

Rooting Research in Mindfulness

13

A Persistent Praxis

Putting Mindfulness Scholarship into Action at Minneapolis College

Jennifer Sippel

The seeds of mindfulness were being planted at Minneapolis Community & Technical College (Minneapolis College) many years before I started working there as a faculty librarian in 2007, and I have been engaged in the efforts to cultivate that garden since about 2012.

I do this work in collaboration with many other practitioners. As a librarian on various teams, I tend to bring scholarship, research, and intellectual curiosity to it. I have had success partnering with the Center for Teaching and Learning (CTL), addiction counseling faculty, health faculty, human resources, and the Office of Diversity, to name a few. In this story, I will talk about my personal journey that led me to Minneapolis College's A Mindful Path toward Equity project.

I was introduced to a formal mindfulness practice around 2005. I was taking a yoga class, which is something I had done many times and for many years. This time, something was different. I found myself being asked to do three things with my mind during the class:(1) stay present with my body, (2) cease judgment of observations made with my mind, and (3) allow the thoughts/sensations observed to move through me with ease. This was the beginning of my mindfulness practice.

I consider 2005 the start of that formal practice, and while I continued to practice yoga, it took me many years before I would participate in my first seated session in 2012. As a busy student/academic/librarian, I found myself saying, "Why would I sit for a mindfulness practice? I don't have time for that! I am too busy doing [important work]!" What I failed to understand then but have learned since is that mindfulness practice cultivates inner peace, which can reduce self-induced suffering and help us sustain habits that allow us to be more present and compassionate for others. It can reduce burnout, increase productivity, and relieve anxiety. A mindfulness practice is not the only way to achieve these outcomes, but it is one way that is available to everyone, just about anywhere.

If I'm being honest, I would say my exposure to contemplative practices goes all the way back to my childhood. Activities like music, worship, dance, theater, and time spent in nature are some of the ways mindfulness was cultivated within me as a child and young adult. However, there are a couple differences between those activities and the mindfulness practices I am engaging and teaching today. One is that those activities often require additional skills or training or equipment. And they are only a formal mindfulness practice if that is the intention going into them. If I am going for a walk in nature but I don't stay present for the walk, that is not a mindful practice.

My search for new literature and techniques continued as I contemplated ways to bring that personal practice into a workplace space where I knew I needed some additional support in order to sustain the hard work I was doing. I wanted to be present and stay present in the challenges with students who were struggling with homelessness, hunger, violence, and poverty, among many other issues. In 2012, I stumbled upon Chade-Meng Tan's Google talk titled "Search inside Yourself" (also the title of his corresponding best-selling book and the leadership institute that formed shortly after). Meng's resources, as well as articles about mindfulness in libraries, launched me into integrating my personal mindfulness practice into Minneapolis College's library and, later on, into my information literacy classes and across the college through faculty and staff connections.

Also in 2012, with the help and support of several colleagues and in partnership with the student life budget committee, I repurposed an old copy machine room in the library into the Room to Breathe: A Space for Mindfulness Practice. As one of the coleaders of Minneapolis College's Center for Teaching and

Learning from 2012 to 2015, I embedded mindfulness into faculty gatherings like teaching circles, book discussion, and development sessions, providing increased exposure and deeper exploration for faculty looking to adopt a practice themselves and integrate mindfulness/contemplative pedagogy into their classrooms and curriculum. CTL has remained a critical partner in the college's mindfulness programs. After several years developing a personal practice, in the fall of 2015, I added guided mindfulness practice into INFS 1000: Information Literacy & Research Skills, a two-credit semester-long class taught by faculty librarians. I have continued to revise this and other courses I teach in Minneapolis College's Library Information Technology program to reflect contemplative pedagogy throughout class sessions, assignments, and assessments.

When talking about mindfulness, it is important to establish a baseline definition for what is being discussed. In order to do this at Minneapolis College, we felt it was important to draft our own definition of mindfulness:

> At Minneapolis College, we believe mindfulness is a skill of intentional self-awareness that cultivates safe and supportive spaces by developing one's ability to bridge difference with thoughtfulness, compassion, and acceptance in the present moment.

Those of us engaged in the work see mindfulness as having applications, as well as limitations, within the domain of equity work. We are still very much exploring what those are and trying to engage in dialogs that include as many perspectives as we do. If you are not familiar, Minneapolis Community & Technical College is a public two-year college located in the heart of downtown Minneapolis, created in 1996 and a member of Minnesota State (the fourth largest system of state colleges and universities in the nation with thirty colleges, seven universities, and fifty-four campuses). Minneapolis College is the result of the merger of two institutions: a technical college with a long history of vocational education dating back to 1914 and an open-enrollment community college established in 1965. Minneapolis College is ethnically, economically, linguistically, and in so many other ways a very diverse campus. In fact, it is one of the most diverse campuses in Minnesota. Of Minneapolis College's student population, 72 percent are underrepresented students. *Underrepresented* is designated as being a first-generation student, a student of color, and/or a low-income student. As a percentage of the total student population, Minneapolis College has had more students of color enroll each year for approximately ten years, with the majority of those students identifying as black/African-American. And while we are leading the system in terms of a diverse workforce, we are nowhere close to having the same diversity as our student body.

As someone who identifies as a straight white woman, I am committed to working on myself so that I can better work on/for equity and inclusion. To me, part of that work involves mindfulness. I want to take a moment to recognize that the term *mindfulness* itself has limitations. For example, during our recent distinguished panel discussion, Rebeka Ndosi referred to mindfulness instead as "healing practices." The term *mindfulness* is, at times, obscured by mass media coverage of the topic and by the commodification of mindfulness (often by corporations), which leads to ideologies such as, "Look, I'm being mindful of equity because I say I'm being mindful," or "I took a two-hour workshop to learn how to be mindful, and now I am." Unfortunately, that is not how mindfulness works. You can't become mindful without ongoing, sustained practice.

In fall 2016, after taking a one-semester sabbatical to deepen my research and practice, I began exploring connections and intersections of mindfulness as part of equity and inclusion strategic priority initiatives at the college. In the spring of 2017, after presenting a pitch with Dr. Jay Williams (Minneapolis College's director of diversity), I was awarded an Innovative Shark Tank Grant for twenty-five thousand dollars to fund a series of programming on the theme "Minneapolis College: A Mindful Path toward Equity." That following summer, I supported the embedding of mindfulness practice into new faculty orientations, equity and inclusion programs, and our presidential discussion series. As part of this grant project, which was originally inspired and informed in part by Minnesota State faculty member Beth Berila's book, *Integrating Mindfulness into Anti-oppression Pedagogy: Social Justice in Higher Education* (2015), we achieved the following:

- At least a dozen Minneapolis College employees were certified as Intercultural Development Inventory (IDI) coaches and are now offering sessions to engage community in cultural fluency professional development plans.

- A customized eight-week mindfulness-based stress reduction (MBSR) class with an equity focus was brought to campus and offered to all employees and students for free.

- Health (yoga, meditation) faculty member Jennifer Mason developed an online course called Mindful Campus Thriving Campus and offered two sessions of the course in the spring of 2018. (The course can also be completed independently but would lack the group discussion aspect.)

- A daylong event called Present in the Hard Work: A Mindful Path toward Equity was programmed for Friday, April 13, 2018, and included a distinguished panel discussion, customized living room conversations, and breakout sessions.

I would also like to point out that mindfulness practices have grown throughout the college in other ways. We are now able to offer at least three weekly guided practice sessions offered in the library's Room to Breathe space, with the possibility of increasing that next year due to growing interest and competence among our staff. An introduction to mindfulness is part of all the new faculty orientations and a core component to the staff development program launched in January 2018. The college president sponsors discussion series that focus on equity and has allowed us space to not only practice mindfulness during those discussions but select readings that investigate the intersections of mindfulness practice and equity work. One of the most important pieces we read this year was a *Teaching Tolerance* article from 2017, authored by Alice Pettaway, "Mindful of Equity: Practices That Help Students Control Their Impulses Can Also Mask Systemic Failures," which included a timely critique of the problems that can result from hasty implementation of mindfulness practices in K–12 settings.

Where is the library in all of this? In addition to providing faculty leadership (me), the college library provides space for practice, has curated several correlating book displays, and has made collection purchasing decisions to support the themes of this work, and we are hoping to provide a LibGuide focused on mindfulness and equity.

Questions we still need to answer include the following: What equity are we referring to? What, if anything, needs to change about our college's working definition? How will this work be sustained into the future? (Right now, much of it has been tied to the grant and/or individual contributions of passionate employees.) How can we get students to integrate into the growing employee leadership on these efforts?

How to get started:

- Adopt a practice.
- Invite others to practice (or explore practicing) with you.
- Present to others about what you are learning from your practice and research.
- Invite others to partner with you.
  ◊ I have found interest in unexpected places/people.

Room to Breathe

◊ The more I engage in conversation, the more people open up to the ideas/concepts they may have been skeptical about.

■ Join local interest groups.

■ Join larger interest groups to network (on Facebook, with ACRL, with local/regional library organizations, etc.).

■ Attend conferences or workshops.

■ Apply for grant funding (more than once).

◊ I have applied for four so far and received two for Minneapolis College Library's Room to Breathe space.

14

Going with the Flow

Finding Flexible *Functionality* in Teaching and Mentoring

Anne Pemberton and Lisa Coats

At the Randall Library of the University of North Carolina Wilmington (UNCW), twenty-five librarians and twenty-seven library staff members serve 16,000 students, 1,333 university staff, and 965 teaching faculty. Providing the best service to our users is always the ultimate goal, but with a growing student body and library resources that have not kept pace, it can certainly be a challenge on any given day! One of the most active areas of service in Randall Library is the Information Literacy (IL) instruction program. The Research and Instructional Services (RIS) department is composed of ten librarians who provide instruction through course-related IL sessions, tours, orientations, and credit courses to nearly eleven thousand users every academic year. With such an active instruction program, it can be difficult to stay mindful, find flexibility, and go with the flow.

As is the case for many academic libraries, teaching is time-consuming, at times exhausting, and often stressful. We have found that practicing mindfulness in all aspects of our positions, but especially in our roles as teaching librarians, has generated a wonderfully positive ripple effect for us individually, for our colleagues, and for the students we teach. Having a consistent, individual mindfulness practice and approach has improved our own personal lives, as well as increased our professional satisfaction, sense of purpose, and specifically, enhanced our teaching experiences.

Both members of the RIS department, we work closely but serve in different roles. As the associate director of Research and Instructional Services and Library Assessment, Anne Pemberton is the head of the department and currently supervises all nine RIS librarians. As the humanities librarian, Lisa Coats focuses on instruction, reference, and liaison duties. As teaching librarians, mindfulness has been an approach we have each used throughout our careers, always looking for ways to remain flexible and incorporate fun into our work. We will tell our own individual stories that share some of the ways we have brought mindfulness into our daily workflow, particularly with IL instruction, which is our mainstay. We will also describe our collaborative work that we are confident has had a positive impact on our colleagues and our students.

Anne's Story

My specific focus of mindfulness is on staying in the present moment. As my career progressed from a boots-on-the-ground IL librarian to the supervisor of nine librarians, I found that no other practice has had as much impact as mindfulness. Like any busy academic librarian, I have days that are booked from first thing in the morning until the end of the day with meetings, classes, more meetings, and more classes. It is crucial for me to stay in the present moment throughout the day. If I am in a meeting or teaching a class and I am thinking about a past moment or planning for a future moment, I have done a disservice to those who are sharing their time with me.

My personal mindful practice is the same as my practice at work. When I feel my attention or thoughts wandering to a past moment or a future moment, I use a phrase (e.g., "Now," "This moment is all I have," "Calm the mind"), or I slow down and focus on my "in breath" or my "out breath." If I am having a particularly challenging day, I make time for a quick meditation. It might be a walking meditation outside or a seated meditation in my office. Typically, I can refocus on the present moment after ten minutes.

Living and working in the present moment lower my level of stress and increase enjoyment of my work. It also benefits those

I supervise, my colleagues, and the students, as each individual gets my full attention and my most positive self. I view every class that I teach as a unique opportunity. There has never been a class like the one I am walking into, and there will never be a class exactly like it in the future. The students, the instructor, the assignment, the day of the week, the time of the day, and the vibe of the room are all unique. I still get nervous when I teach, but I use my phrases, pay attention to my breath, or smile to ease those nerves. Buddhist monk Thich Nhat Hanh has said, "We can smile and blossom like a flower and everyone...will benefit from our peace." I believe that smiling puts me fully into the present moment and can bring a stressed out, busy student who may not want to be in my IL session into the present moment as well. Smiling is a mindfulness practice that calms me and shows students that I am fully engaged with them and that I want to have fun!

I take a similar approach in my role as supervisor. I feel I am most successful and proud as a supervisor when I am fully present in the moment with someone who may be struggling at work, experiencing anxiety about job performance, or running on fumes. I listen to my supervisees with the intention of authentically hearing and understanding. I may not have a solution to the issue at hand, but I am fully engaged with them in the moment. I also believe that having fun is a way to live in the present moment. Sharing funny stories, giving small gifts, and enjoying a tasty treat together are ways that I attempt to bring myself and my colleagues into the present moment.

Lisa's Story

As the humanities librarian, I am a liaison to five distinct and unique departments. It is challenging enough to reach out to the faculty in each of these departments, but being of service to hundreds of students in various programs can, at times, feel overwhelming. I also coordinate our English Composition IL program. Most of these first- and second-year students must take two composition courses, both of which require a face-to-face IL session with a librarian. With five years of previous experience as a First Year Engagement librarian, I quickly discovered the need for focus, coordination, and attention to detail when working with first-year students. I have found that mindfulness is a path to developing these skills and therefore a path to success with my service to students, faculty, and others.

Finding ways to be present and practice mindfulness in the workplace has been an adventure. Being active in library operations and events, participating in department meetings, and collaborating with colleagues calls for consistent soundness of mind and body at work. Using meditation, breathing, and other exercises that help focus the mind on the present moment creates a calm, patient, compassionate, and aware approach. However, practicing mindfulness at work is not enough. Applying it in my personal life is essential.

The main way I practice mindfulness in my daily life is through the acronym HALTS—hungry, angry, lonely, tired, and sick. If any of these dispositions are out of balance, it can affect my entire well-being. Many times, several dispositions need addressing all at once! Eating regularly (that means taking lunch breaks!) makes the difference between a productive meeting or a successful IL class and feeling as though it was a waste of time. I have been committed to eating a plant-based diet and whole foods for well over a decade, which keeps my energy levels high and my mood stable. I have also incorporated yoga, walking, swimming, and other exercises into my life, adding to my overall well-being.

I try to stay aware of my emotional state as well and not dwell on anything for too long. Resentment and loneliness are crippling if not addressed. As Ernest Kurtz and Katherine Ketcham explain in their 1992 book *Spirituality of Imperfection: Storytelling and the Search for Meaning*, "The anger that metamorphoses into *resentment* isolates us." I work to stay in the moment, and if anger arises, I address it immediately and appropriately instead of letting it fester. I read and try to apply ancient philosophies, such as Lao Tzu's *Tao Te Ching*, and more contemporary interpretations like Charlotte Joko Beck's books on living a Zen lifestyle. I also talk to colleagues who help me diffuse anger, which helps me realize that I am not alone.

Just as staying nourished and free of resentment and loneliness helps with my ability to stay present, getting enough sleep can make or break an entire day. However, it can be tough to get enough rest in the midst of the end-of-semester crunch! Homeo-pathic and herbal remedies such as lavender room spray, cham-omile tea, or stress-relief mints help foster a calming attitude when other means have failed or are not available. Likewise, uplifting herbs and homeopathic remedies have given me much-needed afternoon energy. Because all these methods help in my overall health and wellness, I am very rarely sick, which helps keep me engaged and allows my colleagues to rest easy in my dependability.

Our Collective Work

The practices that we both use, while unique to us individually, are all forms of mindfulness. While we are not per-fect, these practices make us better librarians and more peace-ful people. Mindfulness also boosts our confidence in teaching when students may not appear to be engaged. Students who seem more interested in their phones or who blankly stare at you can rattle the nerves of even the most experienced teaching librarian! By practicing mindfulness, we avoid judging some-one's outsides against our insides. Such judgments often lead to feeling like a class was "horrible" when, in truth, the quality of the experience varies for each individual. When we choose how we interpret each session, we fulfill our responsibility to learn from every teaching moment. It is also important to think about the "middle way" in relation to teaching, which is to focus on avoiding extremes and always working toward moderation and balance. As it relates to teaching, classes are very rarely 100 percent "bad" or 100 percent "good," though sometimes we grav-itate toward labeling them as such.

In order to share techniques that work for us, we created and delivered a mindfulness workshop for our RIS colleagues at a departmental retreat. The workshop lasted an hour and pro-vided the following:

- an overview of the concept of mindfulness
- a discussion of the benefits of mindfulness
- examples of how the two of us individually practice mindfulness at home and work

- examples of how the two of us use mindfulness in the classroom to improve our teaching
- a guided exercise from the book *Mindful Eating*
- a group discussion about participants' ideas about mindfulness and their practices

Initial feedback on the workshop was positive, and planning is under way to offer a similar workshop at our next departmental retreat. Broadening the audience of the workshop to library colleagues beyond our department is our goal.

In addition to sharing our practices with our colleagues, we also encourage students to learn about mindfulness practices, primarily through our end-of-semester event called Recharge @ Randall. Guided meditation, chair massage, coloring books, puzzles, yoga, and other exercises have become a tradition at these events. We plan to incorporate more of these activities in Randall Library as we continue to go with the flow and focus on the *fun* in *functional*.

Recommended Reads

Eating Mindfully: How to End Mindless Eating & Enjoy a Balanced Relationship with Food by Susan Albers

Everyday Zen: Love and Work by Charlotte Beck

Living Wisdom with His Holiness the Dalai Lama by Don Farber

Nothing Special: Living Zen by Charlotte Beck and Steve Smith

The Spirituality of Imperfection: Storytelling and the Search for Meaning by Ernest Kurtz and Katherine Ketcham

Tao Te Ching by Lao Tzu

Work: How to Find Joy and Meaning in Each Hour of the Day by Thich Nhat Hanh

15

Overcoming Research Anxiety

A Mindful Approach to Literature Review Searching

Elizabeth Galoozis and Kevin Michael Klipfel

Problem Context

The idea to pilot a new workshop incorporating mindfulness-based practices at USC came about organically after Elizabeth attended a campus event for USC graduate students that touched on the topic of imposter syndrome. *Imposter syndrome*—the psychological fear, prevalent in academia and out, of not measuring up to the expectations of others and therefore being exposed as a "fraud"—can take many forms. Within the context of academic life, it may most often arise as the fear of being not as smart or well-read or even as good at research as one is "supposed" to be, especially in comparison to one's peers or professors. These feelings of fraudulence are often hidden, since the mere expression of one's vulnerability—the exposure of one's imperfections—is a hallmark fear of imposter syndrome. Shortly after attending this campus workshop, Elizabeth and Kevin met to discuss new workshop possibilities. We agreed that helping graduate students overcome some of their anxieties and feelings of fraudulence within our own domain, research and information literacy, might make a great topic for a workshop.

Though creating a workshop aimed at helping graduate students overcome their feelings of not measuring up might initially appear beyond the scope of library work, it seemed natural to us to apply this concept to a relatively traditional workshop offered across academic libraries: how to conduct literature reviews for a graduate thesis or dissertation. The process of gathering information for a literature review can often seem daunting—not just intellectually but emotionally as well. What's worse, many students may feel like they are just supposed to know how to do advanced research and may therefore be afraid to ask others for help (especially faculty members in positions of authority) since they are anxious that this will expose them as academic frauds. This creates a pernicious, self-defeating cycle: we know that we don't know, but our fears prevent us from taking the most meaningful paths to educating ourselves.

We realized that this fear could also be a major impediment to students seeking research help from librarians. For these reasons, two central questions drove our planning around the workshop: Could we design a workshop that helped students overcome these feelings of fraudulence and anxiety around literature reviews? And could we simultaneously help students develop the substantive information literacy skills they'd need to complete their projects?

Designing the Workshop

While brainstorming solutions to these questions, we found reflecting on our own mind-sets and anxieties related to the research process and literature reviews extremely helpful. Our past experiences, combined with our pedagogical knowledge, deeply informed the session's instructional design.

We connected the feelings of imposter syndrome that we initially discussed to the work of psychologist and educational researcher Carol Dweck, whose seminal book *Mindset: The New Psychology of Success* summarizes decades of Dweck and colleagues' research on the ways students' attitudes toward intelligence can impact their motivation for learning. Dweck divides these (often implicit) attitudes into two categories. On the one hand, some of us may approach learning tasks with a "fixed" mind-set: we believe that talents, intelligence, and abilities are "fixed" and that there's not much we can do to improve our abilities in a particular domain. For example, a student who has historically struggled in math courses may come to adopt a fixed mind-set toward learning new mathematical problems; this mind-set may manifest in negative self-talk such as "I'm just not good at math, so there's not much point in trying or putting effort into it."

One way that a fixed mind-set can impact learners is that it often leads to a desire to simply appear smart—or, as is often the case, a sustained psychological effort to not be viewed by others as stupid or lacking knowledge. When considering this research and the consequences of a fixed mind-set, we realized that many students' experiences of imposter syndrome may go hand-in-hand with having internalized a fixed mind-set toward the area of research. They feel like they are supposed to have an inherent understanding of graduate-level research (since everyone else seems to!) and experience anxiety over the process.

This led to the realization that encouraging students to approach research with a growth mind-set—the belief that our talents, intelligence, and abilities are malleable and can be improved over time through sustained effort and feedback from experts—would be a key conceptual element of our workshop that might help our students overcome research anxiety. We've all learned, over time, how to do things like literature reviews, and there's no shame in asking experts such as librarians for help with one's research.

As information literacy educators, we asked ourselves where, specifically, these anxieties seemed to arise for students within the research process. Our goal in brainstorming these stages (outlined in the next section of our story) was to help students develop a mindful awareness of these stages: to identify where they were in the process, understand the attendant anxieties at each stage, and gain metacognitive awareness as to why these anxieties were coming up at these stages. Thus helping our students develop the information literacy skills required to understand the stages of the literature review process was ultimately geared toward helping them approach the research process mindfully.

The Workshop

One of the key tenets of mindfulness is noticing and naming feelings. We started the workshop with an anticipatory set projected on a screen: "Respond to this question on an index card: What emotions does the prospect/process of doing a literature review bring up for you?" We wanted to emphasize this emotion- and mind-set-related framing from the beginning. When we asked if anyone wanted to share what they had written, some students did. Their answers were all along the lines of being nervous or afraid of failing, which conveniently led into our content but also, more important, signaled to us that the students were willing to be vulnerable in sharing their experiences.

The workshop was then framed by four stages that we referred to throughout the workshop, titled "The Evolution of Literature Review Anxiety":

- How do I get started?
- How do I know the seminal works in my area?
- How do I know what's relevant to my search?
- How do I know when I'm done?

These are questions you might find in any approach to teaching or guiding a literature review. Instead of following these questions immediately with strategies, however, we used them to name and explore the more abstract feelings of anxiety on the students' index cards. We emphasized that these are not questions anybody knows the answer to when they are first starting out. We invited students to engage with this uncertainty by acknowledging it as common to all students in their positions. Before addressing the stages with strategies both pragmatic and mindful, we talked about the concept of mind-sets, and asked students to take the "Mind-Sets toward Learning" assessment on Carol Dweck's website. The students seemed to find this valuable and even enjoyable, as they saw different mind-sets reflected in their own results.

This was an opportunity for students to engage in metacognitive mindfulness, to consider how the way they think about themselves as researchers contributes to or inhibits the way they do research. Our goal was to shift students' thinking from "I'm scared this won't be perfect" to "I know this won't be perfect, but here's what I can do to make it good."

Meaningful conversations developed during the workshop, we believe, partly because of how the workshop was framed and partly because of the vulnerability and trust that we both demonstrated ourselves and observed in the students. We shared experiences of our own anxieties and processes around literature reviews, as well as our own experiences with mindfulness, which we related to anxiety as well as information literacy concepts. For example, Kevin told the story of his experience living in residence as a student at the San Francisco Zen Center, where he learned that the practice of meditation involves mindfully paying attention to your breath rather than attaching to the whirlwind of thoughts going on in your head. This narrative built the background knowledge required to introduce students to the concept of mindfulness as an information literacy concept—as a useful strategy for determining the relevance of sources for one's current purposes. During mindfulness meditation, we stay centered in our core while paying attention to our breath. Similarly, during searching, we want to stay grounded in our core research concepts. Doing so gives us the ability to determine what is relevant and what is not: sources are relevant if, and only if, they relate to key elements of one's core research concepts, and they are not relevant when they stray from these concepts. We found this to be a helpful analogy for students to overcome a common frustration during searching: becoming cognitively overwhelmed by the sheer amount of sources they may encounter. By staying grounded in themselves and their core ideas, the process of determining relevance is less daunting; therefore, we expect that introducing mindfulness into the concept of searching will decrease a student's anxiety when faced with potential information overload.

Elizabeth addressed the last stage—"How do I know when I'm done?"—with a story about her own experience conducting a literature review while writing a journal article. She offered the idea of research as iterative and recursive rather than exhaustive (as may be emphasized in guidelines about literature reviews) and talked about noticing things in the process, like the same names coming up, or identifying when a concept seems to have been introduced in a discipline. Elizabeth included an example of her own annotation while searching for sources on library workplaces and generational stereotypes, which was written in plain, stream-of-consciousness language and included what she noticed about a source—namely, that it reiterated points made in other sources and that it was one of many that referred to a specific author, which pointed to investigating that author. She tried to convey the idea that a literature review is never exactly "done" because it is being conducted within a particular time, place, and context.

Throughout, we touched base with the students, asking them for thoughts and suggestions, making their existing knowledge explicit and building familiarity. When we stopped to notice our own thoughts, we both had this one: "This is working."

Our presentation ended with a quote from Twyla Tharp from her book *The Creative Habit*: "Better an imperfect dome in Florence than cathedrals in the clouds." We then asked students to write down one step (no more) that they would take next in their literature review journey. Whatever stage they found themselves in, hopefully they saw themselves moving through the anxiety of that stage with an eye toward the next and a mindful understanding of sitting with where they were in the process at that moment.

APPLICATIONS
Future Directions and Transferrable Elements

Though our story focuses on a particular workshop, we believe that considering our students' emotional lives—and the role mindfulness can play in helping facilitate the research process—can have a significant impact in many areas of reference and instruction librarianship. For one, librarians are in a unique position to address the mindful aspects of research, in contrast to full-semester course instructors. Most librarians present neither stick nor carrot in terms of grades or value judgments; we are there to support students and be as helpful as possible. This allows us to potentially place ourselves in a position of trust with our students, increasing the possibility that students may express their vulnerabilities with us, especially if, as in the case of the workshop outlined in this story, we are aware of this phenomenon and choose to make this affective component of teaching and learning a primary focus of our instruction.

Simply asking our students "How do you feel about doing research?" or "How's the paper going?" rather than moving into a didactic or question-and-answer mode may be one method of going about this in a one-shot instruction session or reference consultation. We have both tried this method of questioning at the beginning of many sessions, often with interesting and pedagogically productive results. For example, asking students what frustrates or challenges them about doing research has led to rich conversations about elements of the research process that we may not otherwise have chosen to focus on, like getting started with a topic or why library services are set up in a particular way.

Focusing instruction around learners' emotions, either as a primary or secondary focus, may be a place of discomfort for some librarians. Librarians may be concerned that we aren't proving our value if we don't supply answers or make judgments. We may be unsure of how to connect with students without crossing personal boundaries. But librarians and students are human beings with emotions, and being mindful of this as instructors can help facilitate librarians' abilities to support the whole student. Acknowledging emotions can help frustrated students adopt a more measured or mindful attitude or can spark connections between research processes and activities they are more familiar with and even like. Perhaps most importantly, it can create relationships between students and librarians, however brief, in which we acknowledge each other's humanity.

Contributors

JENN CARSON is a professional yoga teacher and the director of the L. P. Fisher Public Library in Woodstock, New Brunswick, Canada. She is the creator of the website yogainthelibrary.com and has been delivering movement-based programs in schools, libraries, and museums for a decade. She is the author of *Get Your Community Moving: Physical Literacy Programs for All Ages* (ALA Editions, 2018) and *Yoga and Meditation at the Library: A Practical Guide for Librarians* (Rowman & Littlefield, 2019). She also blogs about her physical literacy adventures at the ALA's Programming Librarian website, programminglibrarian.org. You can find out more about her work at www.jenncarson.com.

MADELEINE CHARNEY is a research services librarian at the University of Massachusetts Amherst. She is an active member of the Contemplative Pedagogy Working Group on her campus and helps facilitate a new campus initiative, Mindfulness for All. She is in the process of becoming a certified instructor of Koru, an evidence-based mindfulness program for emerging adults.

LISA COATS has been the humanities librarian at the University of North Carolina Wilmington's Randall Library for the last two years, having served as the First Year Engagement librarian for five years prior. These positions have provided ample opportunity for engaging in mindful practices to both serve students and faculty and ensure lasting enjoyment in her work. In addition to an MLIS from Rutgers University, Lisa also has a master's degree in English from Virginia Commonwealth University.

JENNY COLVIN, MLS, is the assistant director for Outreach Services at Furman University Libraries, encompassing library instruction, research assistance, the branch libraries, and the library liaison program. She is the liaison to the departments of mathematics, computer science, education, and religion. During the May Experience term, Jenny teaches classes in storytelling and reading. She is a cofounder of the Contemplative Pedagogy Interest Group in the ACRL.

HILLARY FOX is the health, biology, and environmental science librarian at the University of West Florida. In addition to receiving her MLS from the University of North Carolina at Chapel Hill, Hillary has worked with several agencies in North Carolina that support research on the interaction between human health and the environment. Her current research interests include user experience and usability testing, the role of mindfulness in higher education, and embedded librarianship in nursing programs.

ELIZABETH GALOOZIS is head of information literacy at the University of Southern California Libraries, where she focuses on integrating information literacy throughout the curriculum and the university community. She has published and presented on critical pedagogy, library workplace culture, and information literacy and behavior in academic and nonacademic contexts.

LAURA HORWOOD-BENTON is a programming and community relations librarian in New Hampshire and a graphic designer, writer, presenter, and practicing Buddhist. She is the chair of the New England Library Association's public relations committee and has designed materials for NELA's annual conferences since 2015. She presents at conferences in New England and beyond on graphic design, social media, and programming. Mindfulness and compassion are at the core of her work as a librarian.

MILLIE JACKSON is currently senior associate dean at the University of Alabama. She has held various positions at UA as well as Florida State University and Grand Valley State University.

She began practicing yoga and other mindfulness practices in the 1990s. In 2014, she began pursuing yoga teacher training and is a 200-level registered yoga teacher with training from Melissa Scott, Kim Drye, and Becca Impello in both core-strength *vinyasa* and alignment-based yoga. Her love is restorative yoga, however, and she has studied with Jillian Pransky to earn certification. Jackson is also a Certified Health Education Specialist (CHES) and holds an MA in health studies from the University of Alabama.

KATIA G. KARADJOVA is the librarian for the College of Natural Resources & Sciences, the department of world languages and cultures, and the Brain Booth at Humboldt State University. She is a PhD candidate (information science) and holds both an MLIS and MS in physics. Her areas of professional interest/ expertise include information literacy and scholarly research (e.g., in the fields of information literacy, mindfulness and contemplative pedagogy). She values scholarship and presents at several international conferences per year. Her areas of personal interest are poetry and fiction writing, photography, racquet sports, and traveling.

MICHAELA KEATING is the instruction/liaison librarian for scholarly communication at Merrimack College in North Andover, Massachusetts. She received her master of arts in history and master of library and information studies from the University of Rhode Island. Michaela finds quiet contemplation and space for mindfulness between the slow, heavy riffs of doom metal.

KEVIN MICHAEL KLIPFEL is the instructional design and assessment librarian at the University of Southern California Libraries. He is coauthor of the book *Learner-Centered Pedagogy: Principles and Practice* (ALA Editions, 2017), which outlines a person-centered approach to information literacy instruction grounded in educational and Humanistic psychology.

KATHERINE LAFLAMME is the instruction/liaison librarian for graduate programs at Merrimack College in North Andover, Massachusetts. She also serves as the liaison for several undergraduate social science programs. Katherine received her master of library and information science degree from Simmons College.

LISA MELÉNDEZ is an instructional and outreach librarian at Suffolk County Community College. Certified as a yoga teacher in 2012 by the Healing Yoga Foundation, she continues her studies in yoga and Vedic chanting with the Yoga Foundation. Her weekly teaching includes yoga in the tradition of Krishnamacharya, as well as a class for teens with special needs. She regularly offers yoga and meditation workshops at public libraries in both English and Spanish, as well as staff wellness programs.

RICHARD MONIZ is the head librarian at Horry Georgetown Technical College in Conway, South Carolina. Prior to that, he served as director of library services for Johnson & Wales University at Charlotte. Richard was a library director with JWU for twenty-one years. He is also an instructor for the University of North Carolina at Greensboro's LIS program, a role he has held for the past twelve years. He is sole author of the textbook *Practical and Effective Management of Libraries* (2010), co-author of *Fundamentals for the Academic Liaison* (2014), coauthor and coeditor of *The Personal Librarian: Enhancing the Student Experience* (2014), and coauthor of *The Mindful Librarian* (2016), *Librarians and Instructional Designers: Innovation and Collaboration* (2016), and *The Dysfunctional Library: Challenges and Solutions to Workplace Relationships* (2017). He also has a contributed chapter in *Mid-career Library & Information Professionals: A Leadership Primer* (2011) and *Advances in Library Administration and Organization* (2015 edition).

ROBIN O'HANLON is the assistant library director for outreach and public services at the Icahn School of Medicine at Mount Sinai in New York City. In this role, she oversees access services and all library outreach, marketing, and communication efforts. She has a master's degree in information studies from the University of Toronto's iSchool.

ANNE PEMBERTON serves as the associate director of Research and Instructional Services and Library Assessment at Randall Library at the University of North Carolina Wilmington and supervises nine librarians. Prior to coming to UNCW, she served as social sciences librarian at the University of Tennessee and library fellow at North Carolina State University. In addition to her master's degree in information sciences (UTK), she has a master's degree in instructional technology (UNCW).

CARO PINTO is a librarian and instructional technology liaison at Mount Holyoke College, where she works at the interdisciplinary intersection of the arts, the sciences, technology, and the humanities. She has published and presented on critical pedagogy, outreach in special collections, and eportfolios.

MICHELLE REALE is an associate professor at Arcadia University, where she is the access services and outreach librarian. She is the author of four ALA Editions titles, the most recent of which is *The Indispensable Academic Librarian: Teaching and Collaborating for Change* (2018).

KATIE SCHERRER is a consultant, a former children's librarian, and a registered yoga teacher. She is the founder of Stories, Songs, and Stretches! a certification program for library staff, early childhood educators, and yoga teachers that teaches participants to enhance early learning with yoga-inspired movement and embodied play. Katie is also known for her work with libraries and educational organizations nationwide to increase inclusion of Latinx communities in programs, services, and collections. Katie has published two books with the American Library Association: *Stories, Songs, and Stretches! Creating Playful Storytimes with Yoga and Movement* (2017) and, as coauthor with Jamie Campbell Naidoo, *Once upon a Cuento: Bilingual Storytimes in English and Spanish* (2016). More information can be found at www.connectedcommunitiesconsulting.com and www.katiescher reryoga.com.

JENNIFER (JENNY) SIPPEL is a faculty (lead outreach) librarian and instructor at Minneapolis Community & Technical College. She regularly presents on the topic of mindfulness, uses contemplative pedagogy in her classroom, and took a sabbatical in spring 2016 to deepen her understanding of mindfulness in education through research and practice. Most recently, she managed a grant-funded project called A Mindful Path toward Equity, which included a year of programming and training to investigate the intersections of mindfulness within the equity and inclusion strategic priority at Minneapolis College.

REBECCA SNYDER is a library educator, medical trauma survivor, palliative doula, yoga teacher, and loudmouth within the slow medicine and trauma-informed care communities. As an education and instruction librarian for the University of Texas Southwestern Medical Center, she integrates contemplative and critical pedagogies to teach evidence-based medicine topics. She previously served as the library liaison to geriatrics and palliative care for Icahn School of Medicine at Mount Sinai and helped create original contemplative educational programming for Levy Library.

KELLIE SPARKS is the evening reference librarian at the University of West Florida. She is the liaison for the psychology, philosophy and religion, and legal studies departments. Her deep interest in mindfulness and contemplative studies stems from a desire to raise awareness of the library as a calm and welcoming environment for students.

CATHERINE WONG is the instruction/liaison librarian for science and engineering, and health sciences at Merrimack College in North Andover, Massachusetts. She earned an MS in biological sciences from Eastern Illinois University and an MS in library and information science from the University of Illinois at Urbana–Champaign. She is an energy medicine practitioner, and she brings these principles to her daily life and work.

Index

A

"Accidentally Sustainable: Building a Weekly Meditation Community" (Horwood-Benton), 9–15
advertisement, 71
Akombo, David, 47
Albers, Susan, 104
"All It Takes Is 10 Mindful Minutes" (Puddicombe), 73
anger, 102
anxiety
   mindfulness workshop for, 105–111
   writing in journal about, 58
   See also research anxiety
apps
   mindfulness apps, 70
   recommended mindfulness resources, 72
aromatherapy, 47
Association for the Contemplative Mind in Higher Education, 84
Association of College & Research Libraries (ACRL), Contemplative Pedagogy Interest Group, xii

attendees
   of Restorative Yoga sessions, 25, 26
   of Weekly Meditation program, 11–12
attitudes, 106–107
Aura app, 72
awareness
   about research anxiety, 107
   journal, effects on, 59
   relationship to mindfulness, 4
   sharing failure and, 70
   silent technology-free walk and, 87
   of thoughts/interactions, 61–62

B

Be Club, 20
Be Mindful Online Mindfulness Course, 69–70
Be Project
   community, ripples in, 21
   funding for, 19
   idea for, 17–18
   implementation of, 19–20
   lessons for libraries, 22
   results of, 20–21
   team for, 18–19

"The Be Project: Sparking A Quiet
Revolution in Rural Kentucky"
(Scherrer), 17–22
Beck, Charlotte Joko, 102, 104
beginners, 12
beginner's mind, 61, 62
"Beliefs about Meditating among
University Students, Faculty,
and Staff: A Theory-Based
Salient Belief Elicitation"
(Lederer & Middlestadt), 47
Bell, Taunja, 47
Benson, Herbert, 25
Berila, Beth, 94
bicycles, exercise, 33–34
biofeedback machine
for Library Brain Booth, 38–39, 40
popularity of, 41
bird watching kit, 32
blogs, 72
bodhisattvas, 68–69
bookmark, 71
books
mandala coloring pages for Zen
Zone, 47
Mindful McQuade Kit, 31, 32
on mindfulness, library provision
of, 68
recommended mindfulness reads,
104
boundaries, 65
Bowling, April, 33, 34
brain
intentional brain breaks, 38, 39
Library Brain Booth, 37–43
mindfulness practice and, 19
Muse meditation headband
and, 45
physical activity for study, 34
Brain Booth (BB) Initiative, 37–43
Brain Booth Designated Open Space
(BBDOS), 41
Brain Booth LibGuide, 39
breath/breathing
breathing exercises/
visualizations, 64
contemplative practices for
research students, 88–89

impact of Be Project, 20–21
in meditation, 109
reflective journaling and, 59
writing in journal and, 56, 57
Brewer, Judson, 73
Brown, Brené, 18
Brown, Christina, 32
burnout, 78

C
capitalism, 62
Carson, Jenn
about, 113
mindfulness video by, 71
on outreach programs, 67–73
CDs
library provision of, 68
Mindful McQuade Kit, 31, 32
celebration,, 78–80
Center for Teaching and Learning
(CTL), 91, 92–93
Chade-Meng Tan, 92
chakra kit, 32
Charney, Madeleine, xii, 113
circulation, of Zen Zone tools, 51
Clark County Public Schools,
Kentucky, 17–22
Clifton StrengthsFinder®, 75–76
Coats, Lisa
about, 113–114
on flexible functionality in
teaching/mentoring,
99–104
role of, 100
story of, 101–103
coherence, 38–39
collaboration
Be Project, lesson from, 22
for Mindful McQuade initiative,
29–30, 34–35
for Weekly Meditation program, 12
"College Seminar" course, 84
coloring books, 47–48
Color-Relax station, 41
Colvin, Jenny
about, 114
on mindfully managing library
teams, 75–80

Mindfulness for Librarians
    Facebook group, xii
community
    connection with, 22
    impact of Be Project on, 21
    interest in Weekly Meditation
        program, 14
    sangha of library, 13
    sense of belonging with, 69
compassion
    instruction of students and, 62
    in interactions, 61
contemplative practices
    breathing/listening exercise, 89
    childhood exposure to, 92
    contemplative tools in LIB 101
        course, 83–84
    intentional brain breaks, value
        of, 39
    journaling, 84–86
    Library Brain Booth, goal of,
        37–38
    Mindful Medicine program, 3–8
    putting it all together, 89–90
    silent technology-free walk,
        86–88
    student feedback on
        contemplative tools, 88
Continuing Medical Education
    (CME), 6
Coover, Robert, 55
cost, 69
"Craving Quiet: A Library's Zen
    Zone" (Sparks & Fox), 45–52
The Creative Habit (Tharp), 110
creative healing kit, 32
critical thinking, 62–63
"Cultivating a 'Mindful Medicine'
    Ethos" (Snyder & O'Hanlon),
    3–8
curiosity, 66

D
"Dare to Share the Silence: Tools &
    Practices of Contemplative
    Pedagogy in a Library Brain
    Booth" (Karadjova), 39
Davies, Kara, 17–18, 19

depression, 70–71
Destress Fest program, 34–35
Dewey, John, 60
diet, 102
digital resources
    benefits/drawbacks of, 69–70
    list of mindfulness resources,
        71–73
discomfort
    in classroom, acknowledging,
        64–65
    instruction around learners'
        emotions, 111
    reading students' level of, 63
diversity, 94
Doraswamy, Vasundhara, 24
drop-in hours, 41
Dweck, Carol, 106–107, 108

E
eating, 102
Eating Mindfully: How to End
    Mindless Eating & Enjoy a
    Balanced Relationship with
    Food (Albers), 104
"The Effects of Lavender and
    Rosemary Essential Oils on
    Test-Taking Anxiety among
    Graduate Nursing Students"
    (McCaffrey, Thomas, &
    Kinzelmann), 47
Elephant Journal, 72
emotions
    emotional self-regulation, 38
    focusing instruction around,
        110–111
    mindfulness in daily life, 102
    noticing/naming feelings, 108
Empowered Breathing and
    Meditation for Anxiety
    and Stress Reduction
    course, 31
English Composition IL program,
    101–103
environment
    meditation space for Mindful
        McQuade, 30–31
    for reflective journaling, 60

environment (cont.)
  Room to Breathe: A Space for
    Mindfulness Practice, 92–93,
    95–96
  Zen Zone, designated space
    for, 51
eportfolios, 63
equipment
  of BBDOS, 41
  for Library Brain Booth,
    38–39, 40
  for meditation space, 31
  Mindful McQuade Kits, 31–32
  VR, popularity of, 50–51
  for Zen Zone, 46–48, 49–50
equity
  A Mindful Path Toward Equity
    project, 91
  mindfulness scholarship at
    Minneapolis College, 93–96
essential oils, 47
ethics
  library as ethics human library, 8
  mindfulness in medicine, 3–4
events, 14
Everyday Zen: Love and Work
    (Beck), 104
exercise bicycles, 33–34
exercises, 102

F
failures, celebration of, 78–80
Farber, Don, 104
Federico, Danielle, 31
feedback, 48–49
feelings, 108
  See also emotions
fixed mind-set, 106–107
focus, 38
Fox, Hillary
  about, 114
  on library Zen Zone project,
    45–52
fraudulence, 105
functionality, 99–104
funding
  applying for, 97

  for Be Project, 19, 21
  VR, saving funding for, 50–51
  See also grants
Fung Feng, Caroline, 89
Furman University Libraries
  failures/successes, celebration
    of, 78–80
  strengths enhanced through
    reflection, 76–78
  team building, 75–76

G
Galoozis, Elizabeth
  about, 114
  on mindfulness, 61–66
  on research anxiety, overcoming,
    105–111
Game-Relax station, 41
gardening kit, 32
gender reassignment, 7
Giannou, Kyriaki, 47–48
"Going with the Flow: Finding
    Flexible Functionality in
    Teaching and Mentoring"
    (Pemberton & Coats), 99–104
Graham, Linda, 4
grants
  for Library Brain Booth, 38, 41
  for Mindful McQuade initiative,
    31, 34
  for A Mindful Path Toward Equity
    project, 94
  What's Your Ambition?! grant, 19
  See also funding
Greater Clark Foundation, 19
grounding, 109
growth mind-set, 107

H
Hall, Kamerin, 20–21
HALTS (hungry, angry, lonely, tired,
    and sick) acronym, 102
Hamel Health and Counseling
    Center (HHCC), 29–30
Happify, 73
Harris, Dan, 69, 70–71
headphones, noise-canceling, 47

Headspace app, 69
health
    Mindful McQuade initiative,
      29–36
    mindfulness in daily life, 102–103
Hello Humans (podcast), 72
herbal remedies, 103
"Here I Sit . . . By An Open Window"
    (Papoleto), 89
Hey Yo! Yo Soy! Forty Years of
    Nuyorican Street Poetry
    (Papoleto), 89
homeopathic remedies, 103
Horwood-Benton, Laura
    about, 114
    on Portsmouth Public Library's
      Weekly Meditation program,
      9–15
houseplants, 32–33
Howland, Jim, 31
HSU Sponsored Programs
    Foundation, 38
Humboldt State University (HSU),
    37–43

I
imposter syndrome
    concept of, 105–106
    mindfulness workshop, design of,
      106–107
Information Literacy in the Workplace
    (Kurbanoglu et al.), 39
information literacy instruction
    flexible functionality in teaching/
      mentoring, 99–104
    journal writing about, 57–59
    research anxiety, mindfulness
      workshop for, 105–111
INFS 1000: Information Literacy &
    Research Skills course, 93
innovative services
    Library Brain Booth, 37–43
    Mindful McQuade initiative,
      29–36
    Zen Zone, 45–52
Innovative Shark Tank Grant, 94
Insight Timer app, 72

Integrating Mindfulness into Anti-
    oppression Pedagogy: Social
    Justice in Higher Education
    (Berila), 94
intelligence, 106–107
intentional brain breaks, 38, 39
intentionality of practice, 56
Intercultural Development Inventory
    (IDI) coaches, 95
interest, 46
International Conference on
    Higher Education Advances,
    42–43
Internet access, 70
iPad minis, 47

J
Jackson, Millie
    about, 114–115
    on Restorative Yoga, 23–26
job demands-resources
    model, 77
John C. Pace Library, 45–52
journal
    effects of, 59–60
    intentionality of practice, 56
    for mindfulness, 55
    on teaching, 57–59
    time for journaling, 57
    Tree Observation Journal,
      84–86
"Just like Me" compassion
    meditation, 88

K
Karadjova, Katia G.
    about, 115
    on the Library Brain Booth,
      37–43
Keating, Michaela
    about, 115
    on Mindful McQuade initiative,
      29–36
Kentucky, Be Project in, 17–22
Ketcham, Katherine, 102, 104
Kinzelmann, Ann, 47
kits, Mindful McQuade, 31–32

Klipfel, Kevin Michael
  about, 115
  on research anxiety/mindfulness,
    105–111
Kurtz, Ernest, 102, 104

L
LaFlamme, Katherine
  about, 115
  on Mindful McQuade initiative,
    29–36
Lao Tzu, 102, 104
Lasater, Judith Hanson, 25
Lederer, Alyssa, 47
LGBTQQ, 7
LIB 101: Introduction to College
    Research, 83–84
librarians
  library teams, mindfully
    managing, 75–80
  mindfulness scholarship at
    Minneapolis College, 91–97
  mindfulness workshop at USC,
    105–111
  teaching lifelong skills, 90
library
  community of, 13
  mindfulness outreach program,
    67–73
  mindfulness scholarship at
    Minneapolis College, 96
  Weekly Meditation program,
    elements of, 14–15
  Zen Zone, 45–52
library as hub
  Be Project, 17–22
  mindful medicine ethos, 3–8
  Restorative Yoga sessions,
    23–26
  Weekly Meditation program, 9–15
Library Brain Booth
  creation of, 38–39
  mission of/goal of, 37–38
  open space, creation of, 39–40
  research study, 39
  students, impact on, 40–43

library teams
  failures/successes, celebration
    of, 78–80
  managing with mindfulness, 80
  strengths, using to build team,
    75–76
  strengths enhance through
    reflection, 76–78
Lion's Roar: Buddhist Wisdom for
    Our Time (website), 72
literature review searching, 105–111
*Living Wisdom with His Holiness the
    Dalai Lama* (Farber), 104
"Long-Term Music-Listenings' Effects
    on Blood Pressure, Heart Rate,
    Anxiety, and Depression" (Bell
    & Akombo), 47
loving-kindness meditation, 70–71
Lumberjack (student newspaper), 39
Luminosity (brain-training game), 69

M
Madrigal, Justina, 43
management, of library teams, 75–80
mandala coloring pages, 47–48
Manzios, Michail, 47–48
Mason, Jennifer, 95
massage therapy, 67
McCaffrey, Ruth, 47
MCCC (Mountain Comprehensive
    Care Center), 21
McQuade Library, 29–36
medicine, 3–8
  See also Mindful Medicine
    program
meditation
  Anne Pemberton's practice of,
    100–101
  "Just like Me" compassion
    meditation, 88
  Library Brain Booth for, 38
  meditation/mindfulness
    programs, delivery options,
    68–70
  outreach program, interest in,
    67–68

Portsmouth Public Library's
    Weekly Meditation program,
    9–15
Zen Zone, 45–52
"Meditation 101: A Beginner's
    Guide" (Happify), 73
"Meditation Experts Try Virtual
    Reality Mindfulness: A Pilot
    Study Evaluation of the
    Feasibility and Acceptability of
    Virtual Reality to Facilitate
    Mindfulness Practice in People
    Attending a Mindfulness
    Conference" (Navarro-
    Haro), 46
meditation kit, 32
meditation space
    for Mindful McQuade initiative,
    30–31
    promotion of, 34
    Zen Zone, designated space
    for, 51
meditation tools
    VR, popularity of, 50–51
    for Zen Zone, 46–48
meetings, 65
Meléndez, Lisa
    about, 116
    on contemplative practices/
    research process, 83–90
mental health, 29–36
Mental Health Foundation (UK), 70
mentoring, 99–104
Merrimack College, 29–36
metacognitive mindfulness, 108–109
"middle way," 103
Middlestadt, Susan, 47
"Mindful and Reflective Writing as a
    Strategy: How a Work Journal
    Can Help Make You Whole"
    (Reale), 55–60
Mindful Campus Thriving Campus
    online course, 95
Mindful: Healthy Mind, Healthy Life
    (website), 72
Mindful McQuade Kits, 31–32

"Mindful McQuade: Mindfulness in
    the Heart of a Small College
    Campus" (Wong, LaFlamme, &
    Keating), 29–36
Mindful Medicine program
    accreditation of, 6
    conclusion about, 7–8
    creation of, 3
    theme of/resources for, 5–6
    traumatic events, response to,
    4–5
Mindful Mood Balance course
    cost of, 69
    Zindel Seigal as developer
    of, 70
"Mindful of Equity: Practices That
    Help Students Control Their
    Impulses Can Also Mask
    Systemic Failures"
    (Pettaway), 95
A Mindful Path Toward Equity
    project, 91–92, 94
"Mindfully Managing Library Teams"
    (Colvin), 75–80
mindfulness
    Be Project, 17–22
    coming to, personally/
    professionally, 61–62
    contemplative practices/research
    process, 83–90
    definition of, 93
    discomfort and, 64–65
    failure and, 70
    flexible functionality in teaching/
    mentoring, 99–104
    journal writing and, 57–60
    in library, authenticity of, xi
    Library Brain Booth, 37–43
    library teams, mindfully
    managing, 75–80
    limitations of term, 94
    Mindful McQuade initiative,
    29–36
    Mindful Medicine program, 3–8
    A Mindful Path Toward Equity
    project, 91–97

mindfulness (cont.)
Mindfulness for Librarians
Facebook group, xi
at Minneapolis College, 91–97
online mindfulness resources,
71–73
outreach program using digital
resources, 67–73
present moment, staying in,
100–101
recommended reads, 104
reflection/critical thinking, 62–63
research anxiety, overcoming,
105–111
vulnerability and, 63–64
Weekly Meditation program, 9–15
at work, 65–66
workshop for RIS department,
103–104
Zen Zone, 45–52
"Mindfulness Animated in 3 Minutes"
(AnimateEducate), 73
Mindfulness app, 69
"Mindfulness Experiences: The
Library Brain Booth"
(Karadjova), 37–43
Mindfulness for Librarians Facebook
group, xii
Mindfulness for the Academic
workshop, 24
"Mindfulness Is Not a Life Hack"
(Galoozis & Pinto), 61–66
mindfulness-based stress reduction
(MBSR)
class at Minneapolis College, 95
with Mindful McQuade initiative,
29, 30
mind-set
fixed mind-set/growth mind-set,
106–107
noticing/naming feelings, 108
for teaching, 63
*Mindset: The New Psychology of
Success* (Dweck), 106
"Mind-Sets toward Learning"
(Dweck), 108

Minneapolis Community &
Technical College (Minneapolis
College), 91–97
mission, 37
Moniz, Richard, xii, 116
Mount Sinai medical campus, 3–8
Mount Sinai's Center for
Transgender Medicine and
Surgery, 6–7
Mountain Comprehensive Care
Center (MCCC), 21
Mourer, Marissa, 38
multitasking, 68
Muse meditation headband
for Zen Zone, 45, 46, 47
Zen Zone survey results, 49
music
Mindful McQuade Kit, 31, 32
for sound therapy for Zen
Zone, 47

N

Narrative Medicine: A Workshop for
Students and Providers, 5
National Center for Health
Statistics, 67
Navarro-Haro, Maria, 46
Ndosi, Rebeka, 94
Nelson, Allison, 18–19
New England Journal of Medicine, 4
noise-canceling headphones, 47
nonattachment, 14–15
Nothing Special: Living Zen (Beck &
Smith), 104
nyasam (gesture), 88, 89

O

Office of Wellness Education (OWE),
34–35
O'Hanlon, Robin
about, 116
"Cultivating a "Mindful Medicine"
Ethos," 3–8
The Om Place (yoga studio), 18
The On Being Blog, 72
The One You Feed (podcast), 72

one-on-one interactions, 61–62
online resources
  list of mindfulness resources,
    71–73
  on mindfulness, benefits/
    drawbacks of, 69–70
online support, for Be Project, 20
"Outreach for Inreach: Using Digital
    Resources to Promote
    Mindfulness" (Carson),
    67–73
outreach program
  delivery options, 68–69
  interest in, 67–68
  list of online mindfulness
    resources, 71–73
  online mindfulness resources,
    benefits/drawbacks of, 69–70
  online mindfulness resources,
    promotion of, 71
Outreach Services
  failures/successes, celebration
    of, 78–80
  strengths enhanced through
    reflection, 76–78
  strengths for team building,
    75–76
"Overcoming Research Anxiety: A
    Mindful Approach to Literature
    Review Searching" (Galoozis &
    Klipfel), 105–111

P
Palmer, Parker, 57–58
Papoleto Meléndez, Jesús, 89
partnerships
  for Mindful McQuade initiative,
    34–35
  strengths for team building,
    75–76
  See also collaboration
Pemberton, Anne
  about, 116–117
  on flexible functionality in
    teaching/mentoring, 99–104
  story of, 100–101

"A Persistent Praxis: Putting
    Mindfulness Scholarship into
    Action at Minneapolis College"
    (Sippel), 91–97
personal practice
  library teams, mindfully
    managing, 75–80
  mindfulness as not life hack,
    61–66
  mindful/reflective journaling,
    55–60
  outreach program using digital
    resources, 67–73
Pettaway, Alice, 95
Pew Research Center, 70
physical activity, 23–26
physical health, 29–36
Pinto, Caro
  about, 117
  on mindfulness, 61–66
plants, 32–33
podcast, 71, 72
Portsmouth Public Library, 9–15
practice, 22
  See also personal practice
Pransky, Jillian, 25
precarity, 66
pre-existing conditions, 70
Present in the Hard Work: A Mindful
    Path toward Equity, 95
present moment
  finding ways to be present, 102
  staying in, 100–101
productivity, 66
professional development
  workshops, 19–20
promotion
  of Mindful McQuade initiative,
    34–35
  of online mindfulness
    resources, 71
"Providing a Space to Rest: Weaving
    Restorative Yoga into the
    Strategic Plan" (Jackson),
    23–26
Provost Innovation Grant, 31, 34

Provost's Briefing (campus e-mail), 34
publishing, 12–13
Puddicombe, Andy, 73

Q
questions
    about Zen Zone, 51
    Be Project idea and, 18
    reflection questions for Outreach
        Services, 76–78
    space for students to ask, 62–63
    for students about research, 111
    for work journal, 57, 59
quiet
    noise-canceling headphones, 47
    Zen Zone for, 45, 51

R
Randall Library of the University of
    North Carolina Wilmington
    (UNCW), 99–104
Reale, Michelle
    about, 117
    on mindful/reflective journaling,
        55–60
Recharge @ Randall, 104
Reed, Cindy
    on Be Project team, 18–19
    training for Be Project, 21
reflection
    for critical thinking, 62–63
    reflective journaling, 55–60
    strengths enhanced through,
        76–78
    of students on Library Brain
        Booth, 41
relationships, 29–30
"Relax VR" mindfulness app, 46
relaxation
    Brain Booth stations, 38–39, 41
    contemplative practices, student
        feedback on, 87, 88
    Mindful McQuade and, 31, 32
    reflective journaling and, 60
    "Relax VR" mindfulness app, 46
    Restorative Yoga sessions for,
        23–26

Research and Instructional Services
    (RIS) department
    mindfulness workshop for,
        103–104
    of Randall Library, 99–100
research anxiety
    future directions/transferable
        elements of workshop,
        110–111
    problem context, 105–106
    workshop, design of, 106–107
    workshop, details of, 108–110
research process
    breathing/listening exercise, 89
    contemplative tools in LIB 101
        course, 83–84
    journaling, 84–86
    putting it all together, 89–90
    silent technology-free walk, 86–88
    student feedback on
        contemplative tools, 88
resentment, 102
resources
    list of online mindfulness
        resources, 71–73
    for Mindful Medicine program,
        5–6
    recommended mindfulness reads,
        104
Restorative Yoga
    description of, 24–26
    idea for, 23–24
    reflections on, 26
results
    of Be Project, 20–21
    of Zen Zone, 49–50
ripple effect, 99
risks, 78–80
Room to Breathe: A Space for
        Mindfulness Practice
    creation of, 92–93
    guided practice sessions in, 95
    photo of, 96

S
Samsung Gear VR, 46
San Francisco Zen Center, 109

sangha
meaning of, 13
sense of belonging with, 69
of Weekly Meditation program, 13
See also community
Santoro, Jamie, xii
schedule
publishing schedule for Weekly
Meditation program, 12–13
for Restorative Yoga sessions,
25, 26
session timing for Weekly
Meditation program, 11–12
for Zen Zone, 50
Scherrer, Katie
about, 117
on the Be Project, 17–22
on Be Project team, 19
training for Be Project, 21
"Search Inside Yourself" Google talk
(Chade-Meng Tan), 92
Seigal, Zindel, 70
self-doubt, 56
self-regulation, 38
"Self-Transformation through
Mindfulness" (Vago), 73
Seminar and Field Services
Practicum course, 84, 86–87
setup, for Weekly Meditation
program, 11
"Shifting the Pace: Contemplative
Practices and the Research
Process" (Meléndez), 83–90
Shunryu Suzuki, Roshi, 66
signage, 34
silent technology-free walk, 86–88
"A Simple Way to Break a Bad
Habit" (Brewer), 73
singular thoughtful focus, 38
Sippel, Jennifer
about, 117
on mindfulness practice at
Minneapolis College, 91–97
sleep
deprivation, causes of, 23
getting enough, 102–103
smiling, 101

Smith, Erin, 18–19
Smith, Steve, 104
Snyder, Rebecca
about, 118
"Cultivating a 'Mindful Medicine'
Ethos," 3–8
sound, 89
sound healing kit, 32, 36
sources
grounding in core research
concepts, 109
research as iterative, 109–110
Sparks, Kellie
about, 118
on library Zen Zone project, 45–52
speakers, 6, 7
*The Spirituality of Imperfection:
Storytelling and the Search for
Meaning* (Kurtz & Ketcham),
102, 104
stillness, 87
Stop, Breathe, Think app, 72
storytelling
intentional journal, choice to
use, 56
power of, 55
Turn Up the Mic: Reflections on
Experiences with Transgender
Medicine event, 7
strengths
to build team, 75–76
enhancing through reflection,
76–78
stress
MBSR class at Minneapolis
College, 95
of students with research, 83
user surveys for Zen Zone, 48–49
Zen Zone creation, 45–46
Zen Zone, impact of, 49
Zen Zone timing and, 50
Stress Reduction and Mindfulness
course, 31
students
assistants for Library Brain
Booth, 41
Be Project for, 17–22

students (cont.)
  contemplative practices, benefits
    of, 89–90
  contemplative practices, response
    to, 88
  discomfort in classroom, 64–65
  emotions of, focusing instruction
    around, 110–111
  journaling, Tree Observation
    Journal, 84–86
  Library Brain Booth, impact of,
    40–43
  mindful approach of teacher and,
    62–63
  Mindful McQuade initiative for,
    29–36
  mindfulness of librarian teachers
    and, 103
  mindfulness workshop at USC,
    105–111
  of Minneapolis College, 94
  research process, stress and, 83
  silent technology-free walk and,
    86–88
  user surveys for Zen Zone, 48–49
  vulnerability, teaching about,
    63–64
  Zen Zone and, 46–52
success, 78–80
supervisor, 101
supplies
  See equipment
survey
  for Zen Zone, 45, 46, 48–49
  for Zen Zone, review of results,
    49–50

T

Tao Te Ching (Lao Tzu), 102, 104
task shifting, 77–78
teachers
  Be Project for, 17–22
  for Mindful McQuade
    initiative, 31
  for Weekly Meditation program,
    12, 14, 15

teaching
  contemplative practices/research
    process, 83–90
  flexible functionality in teaching/
    mentoring, 99–104
  mindfulness, coming to, 61–62
  mindfulness scholarship at
    Minneapolis College, 91–97
  mindfulness workshop at USC,
    105–111
  reflection/critical thinking, 62–63
  vulnerability in instructional
    situation, 63–64
Teaching Tolerance, 95
Team Strengths Grid, 76
teams
  of Be Project, 18–19
  failures/successes, celebration
    of, 78–80
  managing with mindfulness, 80
  strengths, enhancing through
    reflection, 76–78
  strengths, using to build team,
    75–76
*10% Happier: How I Tamed the Voice
  in My Head, Reduced Stress
  without Losing My Edge, and
  Found Self-Help That Actually
  Works—a True Story* (Harris),
  70–71
Tharp, Twyla, 110
theme, 5–6
Thich Nhat Hanh, 101, 104
Thomas, Debra, 47
thoughts, 61
time
  for journal writing, 59
  session timing for Weekly
    Meditation program, 11–12
  timing for Zen Zone, 50
  for writing in journal, 57
ToDo Institute, 69
training, for Be Project, 21
trauma, 19–20
Tree Observation Journal, 84–86
Tricycle Review, 66

Tricycle: The Buddhist Review
(website), 72
trust, 79, 109
Turn Up the Mic: Reflections on
Experiences with Transgender
Medicine event, 7

U
ujjayi breathing technique, 89
University Libraries (University of
Alabama), 23–26
University of North Carolina
Wilmington (UNCW), 99–104
University of Oxford, 70
University of Southern California
(USC), 105–111
University of West Florida's John C.
Pace Library, 45–52

V
Vago, David, 73
video, 71, 73
virtual reality (VR) goggles
popularity of, 49, 50–51
for Zen Zone, 46
visualizations, 64, 89
volunteers
connection to, 15
for Weekly Meditation program,
10–11, 12, 14
vulnerability
failure/success, sharing by team
members, 79, 80
imposter syndrome and, 105
in instructional situation, 63–64
for mindfulness workshop, 109

W
Waking Up (podcast), 72
walk, silent, 86–88
Warren, Barbara, 7
websites, 72
Weekly Meditation program
for community, 9
demand for, 10
details about, 11

ideas for future, 14
lessons learned, 12–13
replicable elements of program,
14–15
volunteers for, 10–11
what worked, 11–12
WellBAMA, 23, 24
What's Your Ambition?! grant, 19
"When Did Coloring Books Become
Mindful? Exploring the
Effectiveness of a Novel
Method of Mindfulness-
Guided Instructions for
Coloring Books to Increase
Mindfulness and Decrease
Anxiety" (Manzios & Giannou),
47–48
"Why Mindfulness Is a Superpower:
An Animation" (Happily), 73
Williams, Jay, 94
Wong, Catherine
about, 118
on Mindful McQuade initiative,
29–36
*Work: How to Find Joy and Meaning
in Each Hour of the Day* (Thich
Nhat Hanh), 104
writing
after silent technology-free
walk, 87
mindful/reflective journaling,
55–60
Tree Observation Journal,
84–86

Y
yoga
Be project team's experience
with, 18–19
community interest in, 14
contemplative practices/research
process, 83, 89–90
Jennifer Sippel's practice of, 91
in Mindful McQuade initiative,
31, 32
mindfulness and, 68

yoga (cont.)
    people practicing, 67
    Restorative Yoga sessions, 23–26
Yoga and Meditation at the Library:
    A Practical Guide for Librarians
    (Carson), 68
The Yoga Bible (Brown), 32
Yoga in the Library (website), 72
yoga kit, 32
YogaFit-based classes, 24

Z
Zen Zone
    baking times for, 48–49
    creation of, 45–46
    future of, 51–52
    lessons learned, 50
    meditation tools for, 46–48,
      50–51
    survey results, 49–50